CW01559081

ANDALUCIA

TRAVEL GUIDE 2025

LORENA HAMLIN

Copyright © 2025 by Lorena Hamlin.

All rights reserved.

No part of this publication may be reproduced, distributed, or transmitted in any form or by any means, including photocopying, recording, or other electronic or mechanical methods, without the prior written permission of the publisher, except in the case of brief quotations embodied in critical reviews and certain other noncommercial uses permitted by copyright law.

Table of Contents

Introduction

Andalucía, nestled in the southern heart of Spain, is a region that pulsates with life, offering a captivating mix of history, culture, and natural landscapes. From the sun-drenched plains to the snow-capped peaks, the essence of Andalucía lies in its vibrant cities, its fiery traditions, and the warmth of its people. It's a place where the past and present collide, creating an experience that is both timeless and ever-evolving.

The region's warm Mediterranean climate bathes it in sunshine for most of the year, making it a haven for outdoor lovers. Andalucía is a land of contrasts, from the golden beaches of the Costa del Sol to the rugged mountains of the Sierra Nevada. Its cities, like Seville, Granada, and Málaga, offer a heady mix of architectural marvels, flamenco rhythms, and an atmosphere that feels alive with history.

Andalucía is famous for its passionate traditions—flamenco, the soulful dance and music that expresses every emotion of the human heart, finds its home here. Bullfighting, though controversial, is a deeply rooted tradition in the region, a symbol of Andalucía's fiery spirit. And then there's the Andalusian horse, renowned for its elegance and strength, representing a timeless connection between the people and the land.

This guide will take you on a journey through Andalucía's many facets. From its rich historical landmarks to its lively cultural scenes and hidden natural treasures, we'll explore the best this incredible region has to offer. Whether you're seeking adventure in the mountains, indulgence in local cuisine, or an immersion in art and history, you'll find something that speaks to your soul.

This travel guide is designed to help you discover the magic of Andalucía in a way that suits your interests. Each section is crafted to provide insight and practical advice, so whether you're drawn to history, nature, culture, or cuisine, you'll be able to dive into the parts of Andalucía that call to you the most.

Start by exploring the historical gems—places like the Alhambra in Granada or the Alcázar of Seville, where centuries of history are written in stone. If you're a foodie, flip through the pages that delve into Andalucía's culinary delights, from tapas in Málaga to fresh seafood along the coast. For those with a thirst for adventure, we'll guide you through the natural wonders, from hiking the Sierra Nevada to discovering the unique desert landscapes of Tabernas.

The guide is divided into sections to help you plan your trip and make the most of your time in this unforgettable region. We'll cover everything from travel tips to festival schedules, ensuring that every aspect of your journey is as smooth as it is enriching. There's no wrong way to explore Andalucía—follow your heart, and let the chapters of this guide unlock a world of discovery.

From its golden beaches to its rugged mountains, Andalucía has something for every traveler. The region offers not just a getaway, but an experience—a place where the culture and landscape intertwine to create a tapestry of memories that will last a lifetime.

The Sierra Nevada offers skiing in the winter, while the Costa del Sol is a paradise for sun-seekers. In Seville, you can wander through centuries-old streets lined with orange trees, and in Granada, gaze upon the intricate beauty of the Alhambra, a masterpiece of Islamic architecture. Málaga dazzles with its modern art scene and Mediterranean charm, while the white villages of Ronda and Mijas offer a glimpse into Spain's past.

But Andalucía isn't just about what you can see; it's about the way it makes you feel. It's the rhythm of flamenco echoing through the streets of Seville, the flavor of a freshly caught fish grilled right in front of you on the beach, and the warmth of the people who call this land home. It's a place where ancient traditions live side by side with modern life, where every moment feels like an invitation to dive deeper into the soul of Spain.

For those seeking adventure, Andalucía offers hikes, rock climbing, and even paragliding over stunning landscapes. If you're more interested in culture, the region boasts world-class art museums, historic landmarks, and a lively calendar of festivals. Food lovers will find themselves in heaven, with a diverse array of local dishes and flavors that change with every region.

So, grab your book, pack your bags, and get ready for the adventure of a lifetime in Andalucía. Every corner of this region holds something new, something exciting, and something unforgettable waiting for you.

Chapter 1: Andalucia at a Glance

The Heart of Southern Spain

Andalucía, the southernmost region of Spain, is a place where the land feels as passionate as its people. Nestled between the Mediterranean Sea and the Atlantic Ocean, Andalucía's geography is as diverse as it is stunning. From sun-drenched beaches to dramatic mountain ranges, this region offers a landscape that is as multifaceted as its rich cultural heritage.

The Mediterranean coastline, known as the Costa del Sol, stretches along the southern edge of Andalucía. This sun-kissed stretch of land is famous for its golden beaches and vibrant seaside towns like Marbella and Málaga. The gentle waves of the Mediterranean meet the land with soft sandy shores, making it a haven for beach lovers and water sports enthusiasts. The rugged hills that rise behind the coast are dotted with charming white villages, offering stunning panoramic views of the sea below.

To the north, Andalucía is dominated by the Sierra Nevada mountain range. These towering peaks, some of which still hold snow until late spring, provide a striking contrast to the warm Mediterranean coast. The region's highest point, Mulhacén, stands at over 3,400 meters, offering not only challenging hiking trails but also world-class skiing in the winter months. The mountains form a natural barrier, creating microclimates that vary across the region. In these highlands, valleys stretch out below, fertile and full of life. Olive groves are common here, their silvery leaves shimmering in the sunlight, a crucial part of the region's agricultural economy.

Beyond the mountains, Andalucía is dotted with valleys, riverbanks, and vast plains. The Guadalquivir River flows through the heart of the region, nourishing its agricultural lands. It's in these river valleys that Andalucía's famous olive oil is produced, alongside other crops like almonds and grapes. The agricultural richness of the land has shaped the lifestyle of the people here for centuries. It's no surprise that much of the region's cuisine revolves around locally grown ingredients, fresh from the earth.

As you venture inland, the landscape changes once again. The hills grow steeper and more rugged, with limestone cliffs and deep ravines carving through the land. These natural features have been both a challenge and a blessing for the people of Andalucía. The land has influenced everything from the design of the region's homes to its agricultural practices. Many houses are built with thick walls that keep the heat out during the scorching summer months, while the flat roofs help gather rainwater in the region's dry climate.

Speaking of climate, Andalucía is known for its hot, dry summers and mild, wet winters, making it an ideal destination for outdoor activities year-round. Summer temperatures often soar above 40°C (104°F) in the inland areas, while coastal regions tend to be more temperate due to the Mediterranean influence. The dry conditions of the summer months, combined with the fertile soil, make Andalucía perfect for growing the olives that define the region's landscape, as well as for wine production, especially in areas like Jerez and Montilla.

Winters, on the other hand, bring a welcome contrast. While the coast remains mild, with temperatures rarely dropping below 10°C (50°F), the mountains see snow, attracting skiers and snow enthusiasts. It's during this season that the natural beauty of Andalucía truly comes to life—lush, green fields blossom under the cooler temperatures, and the olive groves, in particular, seem to pulse with vitality. Even the Mediterranean climate has its charm, as the region is blessed with occasional rain showers that rejuvenate the earth, making everything feel fresh and alive.

This geography and climate have shaped Andalucía in profound ways, influencing everything from the region's way of life to its unique architectural style. The hot summers and mild winters make it ideal for outdoor exploration. Whether you're hiking through the Sierra Nevada, enjoying the coastal breezes, or strolling through the olive-covered hills, the landscapes of Andalucía offer something for every traveler.

Andalucia's Rich History

The story begins in the distant past, during the Roman Empire. Córdoba, one of the most significant cities in Andalucía, still bears the mark of Roman influence, particularly through the Roman Bridge. Spanning the Guadalquivir River, this bridge has stood for over two millennia and was a vital connection for trade and military movements. Other remnants of Roman rule can be seen in the ruins of the ancient city of Italica, near Seville, where the birthplace of Emperor Trajan still stands as a testament to the empire's reach.

By the 8th century, the course of Andalucía's history shifted dramatically with the arrival of the Moors. The Muslim conquest of the Iberian Peninsula brought a new era of prosperity and cultural development to the region. Under Muslim rule, which lasted for nearly 800 years, Andalucía flourished as a center of knowledge, art, and innovation. Cities like Córdoba, Seville, and Granada became hubs of learning, where scholars translated Greek and Roman texts, making significant contributions to mathematics, medicine, astronomy, and philosophy.

Perhaps the most striking legacy of this period is the architecture. The Alhambra in Granada, with its intricate Islamic designs and stunning courtyards, stands as one of the most iconic symbols of Moorish rule. The Great Mosque of Córdoba, with its famous red-and-white striped arches, is another remarkable example of Islamic architecture that continues to captivate visitors. The delicate blend of Islamic, Christian, and Jewish cultures created a unique artistic and architectural heritage that still resonates in Andalucía today.

However, the tides of history were about to change. The Christian Reconquista, which began in the 11th century and culminated in the capture of Granada in 1492, marked the end of Muslim rule in Spain. This pivotal moment not only transformed Andalucía's political landscape but also its cultural fabric. The Reconquista was a time of conflict, but it was also a period of cultural integration, as Christian monarchs sought to reclaim territory and merge the diverse influences of the region. The stunning mix of architectural styles that emerged from this period, including Gothic, Mudejar, and Renaissance elements, can be seen in the cathedral of Seville and the Alcázar, where Christian symbols intertwine with Moorish designs.

Andalucía's role in Spain's Golden Age is perhaps most famously tied to Christopher Columbus. It was in the port city of Palos de la Frontera, in Huelva, that Columbus set sail in 1492, marking the beginning of Europe's exploration of the New World. This connection to the age of exploration helped propel Andalucía to the forefront of Spain's cultural and economic life. Seville became a crucial hub for trade with the Americas, bringing wealth and prosperity that fueled artistic and architectural development. The wealth of the New World can still be felt today in the ornate churches, palaces, and the golden towers that line the Guadalquivir River in Seville.

By the 19th and 20th centuries, Andalucía had undergone significant political and social changes, and yet, its rich historical layers continued to influence its modern identity. The region's cultural expressions, particularly flamenco music and dance, are direct descendants of the diverse historical influences of Andalucía. Flamenco, with its roots in Gypsy, Moorish, and Jewish traditions, continues to be the pulse of the region, a passionate reminder of Andalucía's complex past.

Today, Andalucía embraces its history while evolving into a modern, dynamic region. Its art scene is thriving, with cities like Málaga becoming known for their cutting-edge contemporary art museums, including the Picasso Museum, a tribute to one of the region's most famous sons. At the same time, festivals like the Feria de Abril in Seville and the Semana Santa processions maintain a strong connection to the region's religious and cultural heritage. Andalucía's festivals, music, and gastronomy continue to celebrate its diverse roots, offering a snapshot of the past woven into the fabric of daily life.

Essential Travel Information

Andalucía, with its diverse landscapes and rich culture, is a destination that can be enjoyed year-round, but knowing when to visit and how to prepare will make your trip even more enjoyable. The region's climate and cultural nuances can vary greatly depending on the time of year, so it's important to plan accordingly to make the most of your experience.

When to Visit

The best times to visit Andalucía are during the spring (March to May) and fall (September to November). These seasons offer the most pleasant weather—warm but not oppressive, with daytime temperatures ranging from the mid-60s to low 80s Fahrenheit (18-28°C). Spring, in particular, brings the region's natural beauty to life, as flowers bloom and the countryside turns lush and green. This is also when many of Andalucía's famous festivals, like Seville's Feria de Abril and Córdoba's Patios Festival, take place. Fall offers a similarly mild climate, perfect for sightseeing and outdoor activities, with fewer tourists than during the summer months.

Summer (June to August) in Andalucía can be incredibly hot, particularly inland, with temperatures often exceeding 95°F (35°C) and occasionally reaching over 104°F (40°C). Coastal areas like Málaga or Marbella are slightly more temperate, but the heat can still be intense, especially in the afternoons. If you do choose to visit in the summer, be prepared for the heat and plan your sightseeing in the cooler early mornings or late evenings. Keep in mind that many locals take siestas during the afternoon, when the heat is at its peak, so expect some businesses to close for a few hours.

Winter (December to February) is also a viable option for travelers, particularly for those who enjoy cooler, milder temperatures. Coastal areas remain relatively mild, while the Sierra Nevada mountains offer skiing opportunities. However, the days are shorter, and some attractions or services may be reduced during the low season.

What to Pack

Packing for Andalucía depends on the time of year and the activities you have planned. In the summer, lightweight clothing is a must. Think breathable fabrics like cotton and linen, sunglasses, and a hat to shield yourself from the sun. Comfortable shoes are essential, especially if you plan on walking around historical sites or exploring the countryside.

If you're visiting during the spring or fall, layering is key. You'll want to bring light clothing for daytime activities, but a light jacket or sweater will come in handy during cooler mornings and evenings, particularly in the mountains. If you're planning to explore the higher altitudes of the Sierra Nevada or other inland areas, pack warmer clothing, even in the fall or spring, as temperatures can drop significantly, especially after sunset.

Don't forget essentials like sunscreen and a reusable water bottle to stay hydrated, especially during the summer heat. A small daypack for carrying your belongings while sightseeing is also recommended.

Local Etiquette and Cultural Norms

Andalucía is a region deeply rooted in tradition, and its locals take great pride in their cultural heritage. Being respectful and understanding of the local customs will go a long way in making your visit more enjoyable.

Tipping in Andalucía is customary, though not always expected. In restaurants, it's common to leave a small tip of around 5-10% if service has been good. For café visits, rounding up the bill is appreciated. In bars, tipping is often done by leaving your change or a euro or two if you've had table service. Taxi drivers also appreciate small tips, though they're not mandatory.

Meal times in Andalucía differ from many other parts of the world. Lunch is usually served between 2:00 p.m. and 4:00 p.m., and dinner often starts around 9:00 p.m. or later. This can take some getting used to, especially if you're coming from a culture where meals are typically served earlier. Be prepared to adjust your schedule and take advantage of the relaxed pace of Andalusian life, where meals are an opportunity to savor, socialize, and enjoy good company.

Respectful behavior is particularly important during festivals or religious holidays. Andalucía is home to many Catholic traditions, and religious sites, like churches or cathedrals, require a respectful tone. Modest attire is recommended when entering these places, such as covering your shoulders and knees. During flamenco performances, it's customary to remain silent and attentive, giving the performer space to showcase their art. Applauding after particularly impressive performances is common, but avoid interrupting the flow of the performance with loud comments or talking.

During events like Semana Santa (Holy Week) or Feria de Abril, the atmosphere is vibrant and celebratory, but it's important to be mindful of the local customs. In religious processions, for instance, maintain a respectful distance and avoid disruptive behavior. These events are deeply meaningful to the Andalusians, and showing respect for their traditions will earn you their admiration and hospitality.

By taking the time to understand the local customs and adjusting your expectations to fit the Andalusian way of life, you'll find that your trip will be richer and more rewarding. The region's combination of natural beauty, rich history, and welcoming people makes Andalucía a truly unforgettable destination.

Fun & Quirky Facts

Did you know that Andalucía is home to Europe's only desert? The Tabernas Desert, located in the province of Almería, is an arid landscape that has been the setting for numerous Western films, earning it the nickname "Mini Hollywood." The vast, rocky terrain may make you feel like you've stepped onto the set of a spaghetti western, with dramatic cliffs and dusty roads that could easily be mistaken for the American Southwest.

Seville, famous for its flamenco and grand architecture, also hosts one of the largest Easter processions in the world. Semana Santa (Holy Week) in Seville is a spectacle that draws millions of visitors each year, with elaborate processions winding their way through the streets. The sheer size of these religious gatherings, with their ornate floats and passionate displays of devotion, is both humbling and awe-inspiring. It's a reminder of how deeply religion is woven into the fabric of Andalusian life.

While most people think of Spain's Mediterranean coast as a sun-drenched holiday paradise, Andalucía's beaches are often a source of inspiration for artists. The light, the colors, and the landscapes along the coast have drawn famous painters like Picasso and Dalí. It's not just the natural beauty but the light itself that seems to have a magnetic pull on artists, capturing a certain magic that you'll only fully understand once you see it for yourself.

Speaking of beauty, Andalucía is also home to wild white horses in the Doñana National Park. These majestic animals, known as the "Marismeno" horses, have roamed the wetlands for centuries. They've become symbols of the park's untamed wilderness and can be spotted galloping across the park's vast landscapes. The horses are as much a part of Andalucía's identity as its olive groves or flamenco dancing, representing the rugged spirit of the region.

In a place as sun-drenched as Andalucía, you'd expect the weather to be consistently hot, but the region is full of surprising microclimates. While the inland areas can reach scorching temperatures in the summer, the Sierra Nevada mountains provide a cool retreat. In fact, the same mountains that offer skiing in winter become a sanctuary from the heat in the summer, with temperatures dipping significantly in higher altitudes. It's a region that offers both sun-soaked beaches and snow-capped peaks within just a few hours' drive.

Flamenco, Andalucía's most famous cultural export, has a surprising and complex origin. Though it's often associated with the Gypsies, flamenco is a blend of several cultural influences, including Moorish, Jewish, and Andalusian folk music. The passionate dance, music, and singing tell the story of Andalucía's turbulent and diverse history, embodying the region's fusion of cultures.

Chapter 2: The Iconic Cities of Andalucia

Seville

Seville is not just a city; it's the pulse of Andalucía, where

history, culture, and passion come together in a perfect symphony. With its winding streets, historic landmarks, and vibrant atmosphere, Seville captures the essence of Andalusian life in a way that few other cities can. Whether you're a history enthusiast, an art lover, or someone who simply wants to immerse themselves in the rhythm of flamenco, Seville has something special to offer.

The Seville Cathedral, one of the largest Gothic cathedrals in the world, is a must-see landmark. It's home to Christopher Columbus's tomb and boasts an impressive collection of religious artifacts. Entry to the cathedral costs around €9, and it's worth every penny. Don't miss the Giralda Tower, originally a minaret and now part of the cathedral. Climbing the tower rewards you with stunning views of Seville's skyline, including the Alcázar and the Guadalquivir River. The price for the Giralda Tower is typically included in the admission to the cathedral.

Just a short walk from the cathedral lies the Alcázar of Seville, an extraordinary palace complex that blends Moorish, Gothic, and Renaissance architectural styles. With its lush gardens, intricate tile work, and grand courtyards, the Alcázar is one of Seville's crown jewels. Admission is around €14, and it's advisable to arrive early to avoid the crowds, as this is one of the most visited sites in Spain. Make sure to leave enough time to wander through the tranquil gardens and enjoy the peaceful surroundings.

Reaching Seville is easy, whether you're arriving by train or plane. If you're traveling from Madrid, the high-speed train (AVE) is a great option, taking approximately 2.5 hours and costing between €30-€70 depending on the class and time of booking. The city also has an international airport, Seville Airport (SVQ), located about 9 km from the city center. From there, you can take a taxi (around €20) or use public transportation, including buses and the airport shuttle.

Once in the city, walking is the best way to experience Seville. Its historic center is filled with narrow, cobbled streets, charming squares, and hidden courtyards. A stroll through the Santa Cruz neighborhood is essential. This former Jewish quarter is a maze of white-washed houses, flower-filled balconies, and quiet alleys. It's one of the most picturesque areas of the city, perfect for wandering and soaking in the atmosphere. The neighborhood also offers plenty of cafes, where you can stop and enjoy a refreshing drink or some tapas.

Speaking of tapas, Seville is renowned for its food scene. The city's tapas bars are some of the best in Spain, and trying local specialties is an absolute must. You'll find everything from rich Iberian ham to fried fish, all served in small, shareable portions. A typical tapas meal will cost around €20-€30, but prices can vary depending on where you choose to eat. For a more elevated experience, head to one of Seville's Michelin-starred restaurants, where the tapas are presented with a contemporary twist.

Flamenco, the passionate and fiery dance, is the heart of Seville's cultural identity. There's no better place to experience it than in the city's traditional tablaos, intimate venues where local performers bring the music to life. Tickets for a flamenco show range from €20-€40, depending on the venue and whether you're enjoying a meal with the performance. Whether you choose a dinner show or a more casual performance, the experience will be unforgettable. The rhythm of the guitar, the stomping of the dancer's feet, and the soulful singing will give you a deep sense of Andalucía's rich cultural heritage.

Seville is also famous for its festivals, particularly Semana Santa (Holy Week) and Feria de Abril (April Fair). Semana Santa is one of the most important religious celebrations in Spain, drawing crowds from all over the world. During this week, elaborate processions wind through the streets, with religious statues carried by members of local brotherhoods. It's a deeply moving and visually stunning experience, though it's also a time when the city can get very crowded. The Feria de Abril, held two weeks after Semana Santa, is a joyous celebration of Andalusian culture, with flamenco dancing, horse parades, and an abundance of food and drink. The fairgrounds come alive with colorful tents (casetas), where locals gather to eat, drink, and dance.

Seville's importance in Andalusian culture cannot be overstated. From its stunning monuments to its festivals and food, the city encapsulates the spirit of Andalucía. It's a place where history and tradition meet modern life, creating a dynamic and welcoming environment for visitors.

Granada

Granada, the jewel of Andalucía, is a city that captivates with its  rich history, stunning landscapes, and deep Moorish roots. At the heart of this enchanting destination lies the Alhambra, a UNESCO World Heritage site and one of Spain's most iconic monuments. The Alhambra, with its intricate Islamic architecture and beautiful gardens, is a symbol of the cultural fusion that shaped the city over centuries. Visiting Granada is not just about seeing the Alhambra—it's about stepping into a city where the past and present coexist harmoniously.

The Alhambra is undoubtedly the highlight of any visit to Granada. Admission prices range from €14 to €20, depending on the time of year, and it's highly recommended to book tickets in advance to avoid long lines and guarantee entry. The Alhambra is one of the most visited sites in Spain, and pre-booking ensures a smoother experience. Tickets are sold with timed entries, so be sure to plan accordingly. You can reach the Alhambra either by bus or on foot from the city center, though walking through the historic Albaicín district provides a unique experience. The Albaicín is a maze of narrow, whitewashed streets that once served as the heart of Granada's Moorish community, and wandering through its winding alleys gives you a real sense of the city's rich heritage.

Once inside the Alhambra, the site reveals a breathtaking combination of architecture, history, and nature. The Nasrid Palaces are the most famous part, with their detailed tile work, delicate stucco carvings, and grand courtyards. The Generalife Gardens, a tranquil paradise of fountains, pools, and fragrant flowers, offer a peaceful contrast to the ornate palaces. It's easy to spend hours here, marveling at the beauty of the Alhambra and imagining what life must have been like for the last Muslim rulers of Spain. Be sure to take in the panoramic views of Granada from the Alhambra's towers, where the red-tiled roofs and narrow streets of the city stretch out before you, framed by the backdrop of the Sierra Nevada mountains.

One of the best spots to take in views of the Alhambra is the Mirador de San Nicolás, located in the Albaicín district. From here, you'll get one of the most iconic views of the Alhambra, with the snow-capped peaks of the Sierra Nevada in the distance. It's a great spot for photographs, especially at sunset when the light casts a warm glow on the Alhambra's red walls.

Getting around Granada is relatively easy, with several public transport options available. Buses are the most affordable and convenient way to travel within the city, though taxis are also widely available for a more direct route. The funicular to the Alhambra is another great option, offering a quick ride up the hill and avoiding the steep climb. If you're staying in the city center, walking is often the best way to explore Granada's charms up close, as many of the city's most important landmarks are within walking distance of each other.

One of Granada's most unique aspects is its food culture, particularly the famous free tapas that accompany drinks at most local bars. Order a drink, and you'll be treated to a complimentary tapa, ranging from savory olives to a delicious plate of jamón or a mini seafood paella. This "tapas culture" makes Granada an affordable destination for food lovers, as you can easily have a satisfying meal without breaking the bank. The tapas offerings vary depending on the bar, so it's worth hopping between a few to sample different regional specialties.

For those looking to explore beyond the city, Granada is surrounded by natural beauty. The nearby Sierra Nevada mountains offer fantastic opportunities for hiking, skiing, and snowboarding. In the winter months, the ski resort attracts visitors from all over Europe, while in the warmer months, the mountains are perfect for hiking, mountain biking, and enjoying the breathtaking views of the surrounding countryside. The natural diversity around Granada provides an ideal balance to the urban beauty of the Alhambra, offering outdoor enthusiasts plenty of ways to connect with nature.

Granada's blend of Islamic heritage, stunning architecture, and vibrant culture makes it one of the most captivating cities in Spain. The Alhambra, with its intricate artistry and historical significance, serves as the perfect symbol of the city's past, while the charming streets, free tapas, and nearby mountains invite visitors to enjoy everything Granada has to offer.

Cordoba

Córdoba, a city where the ancient and the contemporary coexist in perfect harmony, offers a truly unique experience for visitors.

Known for its monumental Mezquita-Catedral, the city is a treasure trove of history, culture, and art, but also a thriving modern hub with plenty to explore. Whether you're wandering through its narrow, winding streets or admiring its blend of Roman, Moorish, and Christian heritage, Córdoba will leave you enchanted.

Getting to Córdoba is easy, especially from Seville, which is just  40 minutes away by train. Trains run frequently throughout the day, and tickets range from €15 to €30, depending on the time of day and how early you book. Once you arrive at Córdoba's train station, you're only a short distance from the heart of the city, where most of the main attractions are located. To explore the city, walking is highly recommended, as it allows you to wander through the charming streets of the Jewish Quarter and discover hidden gems tucked away in every corner. Alternatively, if you're not in the mood for walking, the city's efficient local bus system can take you between major sights, and you can also opt for bike rentals, which are an affordable and fun way to see the city.

The city's star attraction is undoubtedly the Mezquita-Catedral, a mosque-turned-cathedral that dates back to the 8th century. This architectural wonder reflects Córdoba's role as one of the most important cities in medieval Spain under Muslim rule. The Mezquita's vast interior, with its iconic red-and-white striped arches and forest of columns, is unlike anything you'll see elsewhere. A visit costs €10, and while it's possible to visit the

Mezquita at any time, early mornings and late afternoons tend to be less crowded, giving you a more peaceful experience. It's a place that feels timeless, with every stone telling a story of cultural fusion and religious history.

Córdoba's other historical landmarks are equally impressive. The Roman Bridge, which spans the Guadalquivir River, dates back to the 1st century BC and is a stunning example of ancient engineering. From here, you can enjoy views of the Mezquita-Catedral and the city's picturesque old town. The Alcázar de los Reyes Cristianos, a fortified palace with beautiful gardens, is another must-see. This former royal residence offers a glimpse into Córdoba's Christian past and provides a tranquil spot to relax amidst its leafy courtyards and fountains.

In addition to its historical gems, Córdoba has embraced modernity with open arms. The Calahorra Tower, located at the far end of the Roman Bridge, houses a fascinating museum that highlights the city's diverse cultural heritage. The Viana Palace, a charming 14th-century mansion, also stands as a testament to Córdoba's rich past while offering a contemporary art collection in its stunning courtyards. These modern attractions are just as integral to understanding the full scope of the city's evolution.

One of the most delightful experiences in Córdoba is the famous Patio Festival, held every May, when the city's private courtyards open their doors to the public. During the festival, the patios are decorated with vibrant flowers and plants, creating a beautiful and fragrant display. Even outside of the festival, Córdoba's patios are worth seeking out, as many local homes feature these intimate spaces filled with greenery, offering a peaceful escape from the city's bustle.

Of course, no visit to Córdoba would be complete without sampling its culinary delights. One of the city's most famous dishes is salmorejo, a cold, refreshing tomato-based soup that's perfect for Córdoba's warm climate. You'll find this dish served in almost every restaurant or tapas bar. For an authentic experience, head to a traditional tavern like Bodegas Campos, where you can pair your salmorejo with local wines and other Andalusian specialties. The city's food scene is relaxed and welcoming, and with many restaurants offering outdoor seating, it's a great place to enjoy a leisurely meal while taking in the sights.

Córdoba's relatively small size makes it easy to navigate, and with bike rentals available for as little as €5 per day, it's an affordable and eco-friendly way to explore the city. Whether you're cycling along the river or leisurely strolling through the historic center, you'll be able to see the city's most important landmarks while enjoying the warm Andalusian sunshine.

In Córdoba, history is not confined to museums or monuments—it's part of the everyday life of the city. From the ancient ruins to the vibrant flower-filled patios, this city perfectly balances the old and the new, inviting visitors to delve deep into its fascinating past while also enjoying the comforts and charm of modern Spain.

Malaga

Málaga, with its Mediterranean charm, is a city that perfectly captures the essence of the Costa del Sol—sun, sea, culture, and an easygoing lifestyle. Whether you're lounging on golden beaches, exploring its rich cultural offerings, or indulging in fresh seafood, Málaga seamlessly blends the laid-back vibe of southern Spain with its dynamic artistic scene.

One of Málaga's most inviting features is its proximity to the  beach. Playa de la Malagueta, the city's most famous beach, is just a 10-minute walk from the city center. With its soft sands, crystal-clear waters, and beachside chiringuitos (bars), it's the perfect spot to unwind after a day of sightseeing. The Mediterranean climate makes it easy to enjoy the outdoors year-round, and many other beaches along the coastline, such as Playa del Palo, offer quieter alternatives with a more local feel.

But Málaga is far more than just a beach destination. It is a cultural haven, with a vibrant art scene that will captivate art lovers and history enthusiasts alike. The Picasso Museum is one of the city's highlights, offering an impressive collection of works by Málaga's most famous son, Pablo Picasso. The museum provides a fascinating insight into the evolution of Picasso's style, from his early works to his later, more abstract pieces. Tickets to the museum cost around €9, and it's a must-visit for anyone with an appreciation for modern art. The Centro Pompidou Málaga is another gem, housed in a striking glass cube. It brings the avant-garde art scene of Paris to Málaga, with rotating exhibitions and contemporary art collections that reflect the city's growing role as an art capital.

Málaga's Soho district adds a more urban twist to the art experience. This neighborhood is a canvas for street art, where murals and installations pop up on nearly every corner, transforming ordinary buildings into pieces of contemporary art. It's a great place to wander, camera in hand, and discover the unexpected pieces that give the city its modern, creative edge.

Getting to Málaga is easy, especially if you're coming from Seville, where a direct train ride takes about 2 hours and costs between €20 and €50. Málaga's main train station, María Zambrano, is well-connected to the city center by bus or a quick taxi ride. Once in the city, getting around is a breeze. The public transport system is affordable and efficient, with buses and a metro line connecting most parts of the city. If you prefer to explore on foot, Málaga's compact city center makes it ideal for walking, allowing you to easily hop between cultural sights, cafés, and the beach.

For those looking for panoramic views of the city, a visit to the Alcázaba fortress and Gibralfaro Castle is essential. The Alcázaba, a Moorish palace-fortress that dates back to the 11th century, is perched on a hill overlooking the city. Its lush gardens, ancient walls, and scenic courtyards provide a glimpse into Málaga's Islamic past. From the Alcázaba, you can take a short hike up to the Gibralfaro Castle, which offers breathtaking views of Málaga, the Mediterranean, and the surrounding mountains. The combined ticket for both attractions is around €5, making it a great value for the incredible vistas and historical insight.

Málaga's culinary scene is just as diverse as its cultural offerings. For a taste of the Mediterranean, head to one of the city's many seafood restaurants, where fresh fish and shellfish are served daily. A local specialty to try is espeto de sardinas, a dish consisting of sardines skewered on a metal rod and grilled over an open flame. The fish is then served with a drizzle of olive oil and a squeeze of lemon—a simple yet flavorful dish that's a favorite among locals. Dining in Málaga is a relaxed affair, with many restaurants offering outdoor seating where you can enjoy the warm evening breeze while sampling regional delicacies.

For those looking to venture beyond the city, Málaga serves as a great base for day trips. One popular destination is Nerja, a coastal town about an hour's drive from Málaga. Famous for its crystal-clear waters and dramatic cliffs, Nerja offers beautiful beaches and the famous Nerja Caves, a network of prehistoric caverns with impressive stalactites and cave paintings. Alternatively, the picturesque town of Ronda, perched on a dramatic gorge, is another great option. Ronda is known for its stunning views, historic bullring, and charming old town, making it an ideal escape for those seeking a taste of traditional Andalusia.

Málaga's blend of sun, sea, and art makes it an irresistible destination for travelers. The combination of its relaxed Mediterranean lifestyle and vibrant cultural scene ensures that a visit to Málaga is as enriching as it is enjoyable.

Cadiz

Cádiz, one of the oldest continuously inhabited cities in Europe, has over 3,000 years of history etched into its very streets. Located on a narrow peninsula jutting into the Atlantic Ocean, the city's history is intimately tied to its position as an ancient seaport. Founded by the Phoenicians, it later flourished under the Romans and Moors, and its strategic coastal location made it an important port throughout the ages. Today, Cádiz still holds onto much of its historic charm, with ancient walls, stunning viewpoints, and a vibrant atmosphere that blends old-world character with modern energy.

One of the most iconic landmarks in Cádiz is the Cádiz Cathedral,  a grand structure that overlooks the city's main square. Built over a period of more than a century, the cathedral mixes Baroque and Neoclassical styles, creating a stunning visual experience. Admission to the cathedral costs around €5, and visitors can also climb to the top of its bell tower for panoramic views of the city and the sea beyond. Another must-see is the Torre Tavira, an 18th-century watchtower offering sweeping views over Cádiz. The tower is home to the Camera Obscura, an optical device that offers a real-time, 360-degree view of the city. A ticket to Torre Tavira costs about €7, making it an affordable and memorable way to experience Cádiz from above.

To reach Cádiz, the most convenient way is to take a train from Seville. The journey takes around 1.5 hours, and tickets range from €10 to €20 depending on the class and time of booking. Buses are also available and take about the same amount of time, though the train offers a more comfortable ride and scenic views along the way. Once you arrive in Cádiz, you'll find that the city is best explored on foot. Its narrow, labyrinthine streets are perfect for wandering, with hidden squares, local cafés, and vibrant markets around every corner. The city's compact size makes it easy to visit its key attractions without needing much public transport, though local buses are available if you want to venture further.

Cádiz's coastal lifestyle is one of its defining features. The city is surrounded by beautiful beaches, and Playa de la Victoria is the most popular for sunbathing and swimming. Stretching for miles, this golden sand beach offers plenty of space to relax, and the nearby promenade is lined with restaurants and bars where you can enjoy a refreshing drink with a view. The Mediterranean climate ensures warm weather year-round, making Cádiz a fantastic destination whether you're seeking a summer escape or a mild winter retreat.

Cádiz's cuisine is another highlight. As a coastal city, it's no surprise that seafood plays a central role in local dishes. One of the must-try foods is tortillitas de camarones, or shrimp fritters. These crispy, golden fritters are made with tiny shrimp and chickpea flour, and they're a popular snack in local bars and restaurants. Another seafood delicacy to sample is pescaíto frito, a dish of small, deep-fried fish, often served with a squeeze of lemon and a side of aioli. For a true taste of Cádiz, head to one of the city's bustling seafood markets, such as Mercado Central, where you can watch the fishmongers at work and pick up fresh seafood for a picnic or meal.

If you're in Cádiz during Carnival (usually held in February or March), you're in for an unforgettable experience. Cádiz's Carnival is one of the most famous in Spain, with extravagant costumes, colorful parades, and lively street performances that fill the entire city. Locals and visitors alike take part in the festivities, with the streets becoming a vibrant mix of music, dancing, and revelry. If you plan to visit during Carnival, be prepared for large crowds and book your accommodation well in advance, as the city is a popular destination during this time. It's a celebration of Cádiz's unique spirit and a perfect opportunity to experience the city's joyful, carefree energy.

For a more serene experience, consider taking a boat tour to see Cádiz from the sea. There are plenty of companies offering guided boat trips around the bay, allowing you to appreciate the city's historic walls, the port, and the coastline from a completely different perspective. A boat tour is a great way to relax while soaking in the scenery and learning more about the city's maritime heritage.

Cádiz's blend of history, coastal charm, and vibrant atmosphere makes it a unique destination in Andalucía. With its rich cultural heritage, bustling markets, and lively festivals, Cádiz continues to be a city that honors its past while embracing the energy of modern life.

Jerez de la Frontera

Jerez de la Frontera, a charming city in the heart of Andalucía, is  synonymous with three things: sherry wine, Andalusian horses, and flamenco. It's a place where history, tradition, and passion come together in perfect harmony. Jerez offers an authentic Andalusian experience that immerses you in its unique cultural heritage, making it a must-visit for those exploring the region.

To get to Jerez, traveling by train from Seville is an easy and scenic option. The journey takes about an hour, with tickets ranging from €10 to €15. Once you arrive in Jerez, you'll find the city's attractions within easy reach, either by foot or with a quick ride on public transport. The city is compact, making it perfect for strolling through its historic streets, which are filled with beautiful architecture and a laid-back atmosphere.

Jerez's sherry wine is world-famous, and no visit is complete without touring one of its prestigious bodegas. González Byass, one of the most renowned sherry producers, offers an excellent tour starting at €10. The tour will take you through the bodega's historic cellars, where you'll learn about the intricate process of sherry production and the rich history of the González Byass family. You'll also have the chance to taste a variety of sherries, from the dry Fino to the rich, sweet Pedro Ximénez. Another notable bodega is Bodegas Tío Pepe, where you can experience similar tours and tastings in a picturesque setting. For wine enthusiasts or those simply curious about the craft, these tours offer a fantastic introduction to the world of sherry.

Jerez is also famous for its Andalusian horses, which are considered some of the finest in the world. The Royal Andalusian School of Equestrian Art is where visitors can witness the beauty and precision of the Andalusian horse in action. The school offers daily shows that showcase the horses' grace, strength, and training. Tickets for the equestrian performances range from €18 to €30, depending on the show. These performances are an impressive display of skill and tradition, often accompanied by classical music and the beautiful choreography of the riders. The school itself is also worth a visit for anyone interested in equestrian arts, as its grounds are a testament to the region's deep-rooted horse culture.

Flamenco is another cornerstone of Jerez's identity. Known as the birthplace of flamenco, Jerez is where this passionate art form thrives, and the city is home to some of the best flamenco shows in Spain. One popular venue is Tablao Flamenco El Templo, where you can enjoy an intimate, high-energy performance by talented dancers, singers, and musicians. Tickets typically range from €25 to €50, depending on the show and whether you choose to enjoy dinner along with the performance. Watching flamenco in Jerez is a mesmerizing experience, as the city's deep connection to the art form adds an emotional intensity to the performances that is hard to find elsewhere.

Aside from its cultural highlights, Jerez de la Frontera also boasts a beautiful historic center, where you can wander through narrow streets lined with whitewashed buildings and flower-filled balconies. One of the key landmarks is the Alcázar of Jerez, a Moorish fortress that offers sweeping views of the city. Another notable site is the Jerez Cathedral, an impressive mix of Gothic and Baroque architecture. The historic center is full of charming squares and cafés, perfect for stopping to relax and enjoy the Andalusian sunshine.

The countryside surrounding Jerez is equally inviting, with rolling hills and vineyards that produce the region's famous wines. If you have time, consider taking a short drive to explore the nearby rural areas. The landscapes here are ideal for scenic walks or bike rides, and you'll often come across small, family-owned wineries where you can stop for a tasting.

No trip to Jerez would be complete without sampling its local cuisine. One of the standout dishes is rabo de toro, a rich oxtail stew that's slow-cooked to perfection with red wine, vegetables, and spices. It's a comforting, flavorful dish that embodies the rustic side of Andalusian cooking. Other local specialties include pescaíto frito (fried fish), which you can enjoy at one of the many seafood restaurants in the city, and flamenquín, a deep-fried meat roll that's a popular snack or main course.

Jerez de la Frontera is a city that invites you to experience Andalucía in its truest form. From sherry tastings to equestrian shows, flamenco performances, and delicious food, the city offers a rich tapestry of experiences that reflect the soul of the region.

Chapter 3: Andalucia's Natural Wonders

The Sierra Nevada

The Sierra Nevada mountain range is one of Spain's most awe-inspiring natural landscapes, offering dramatic vistas and a diverse range of outdoor activities throughout the year. Stretching across the region of Andalucía, the range is home to some of the highest peaks in the country, including Mulhacén, which at 3,479 meters stands as the highest mountain in mainland Spain. This towering mountain, along with its surrounding peaks, creates a rugged, breathtaking environment that attracts adventurers, nature lovers, and anyone seeking to experience the raw beauty of the Spanish landscape.

In the winter, the Sierra Nevada is transformed into a paradise for snow sports enthusiasts. The Sierra Nevada Ski Resort, located at the foot of the mountains, offers some of the best skiing and snowboarding conditions in Europe. With over 100 kilometers of slopes and snow coverage from December to April, the resort is a top destination for both beginner and expert skiers. A lift pass at the resort costs between €40 and €55 per day, depending on the season, giving visitors access to a range of slopes and snow parks. The resort also has excellent facilities for snowboarding and other winter sports, making it an ideal destination for anyone looking to embrace the snow-capped mountains.

But the Sierra Nevada is far more than a winter sports destination. In the summer months, the mountains come alive with hiking, mountaineering, and wildlife watching. The warmer weather reveals a completely different side of the Sierra Nevada, where alpine meadows, crystal-clear lakes, and ancient pine forests create a perfect environment for outdoor exploration. Hiking is a popular activity here, with trails catering to all levels of experience. One of the most famous trails is the Vereda de la Estrella, a well-known route that offers stunning panoramic views of the surrounding mountains and valleys. This trail is relatively moderate in difficulty and takes you through beautiful landscapes, including lush valleys and rocky outcrops, with views of Mulhacén looming in the distance. Best of all, it's free to access, making it an ideal hike for those looking to immerse themselves in nature without any added costs.

For those interested in mountaineering, the Sierra Nevada offers challenging climbs, including the ascent of Mulhacén itself. This hike requires some experience, as the high altitude and rocky terrain present a more demanding challenge. Reaching the summit is a rewarding experience, providing a panoramic view of the entire range and the surrounding region. There are also plenty of other routes for climbers of various skill levels, from easy strolls to more strenuous climbs.

In addition to outdoor activities, the Sierra Nevada has been designated a UNESCO Biosphere Reserve due to its remarkable biodiversity. The range is home to a wealth of plant and animal species, many of which are endemic to the area. Rare species such as the Spanish ibex, the mountain goat, and the golden eagle can be spotted in the higher regions, while the lower valleys are home to a variety of Mediterranean plants and wildlife. Birdwatchers and nature enthusiasts will find plenty to explore, with the opportunity to see a wide range of wildlife in their natural habitat.

Getting to the Sierra Nevada is easy, with the nearest major city being Granada, just a 30-minute drive or bus ride away. Granada offers a wealth of historical and cultural attractions, including the iconic Alhambra, and makes for a great base for those visiting the mountains. There are several transport options from Granada to the Sierra Nevada Ski Resort, including buses that run frequently during the winter months. For those driving, the mountain roads are well-maintained, though it's always a good idea to check the weather conditions in winter before heading up, as snow and ice can make driving more challenging.

For accommodation, the Sierra Nevada and nearby Granada offer a wide range of options to suit different preferences and budgets. In the mountain village of Pradollano, close to the ski resort, you'll find cozy lodges and chalets that provide a rustic, alpine experience. These are ideal for visitors wanting to be close to the slopes or hiking trails. For those preferring a more luxurious stay, Granada offers high-end hotels with stunning views of the mountains and easy access to the city's attractions. Whether you're looking for a charming mountain retreat or a luxurious hotel in the heart of Granada, there are accommodations to fit every need.

The Sierra Nevada is a destination that offers something for everyone—whether you're looking to ski down the slopes in winter, hike through pristine alpine meadows in summer, or simply relax in the midst of Spain's most breathtaking natural scenery. With its stunning peaks, rich biodiversity, and proximity to Granada, the Sierra Nevada is a must-visit for anyone seeking adventure, tranquility, or simply a deeper connection with nature.

Doñana National Park

Doñana National Park, a UNESCO World Heritage site, is one of  Europe's most important and diverse natural reserves, renowned for its exceptional birdwatching opportunities. Located in southwestern Spain, near the Guadalquivir River, the park is home to an impressive range of ecosystems, including wetlands, dunes, forests, and salt marshes. This unique blend of habitats creates a perfect environment for a wide variety of wildlife, particularly birds. For birdwatchers, Doñana is nothing short of a paradise, with its diverse species and strategic position along migratory routes.

The park's diverse landscapes play a key role in its appeal. The vast marshes, with their shallow waters and reed beds, are perfect for aquatic birds, while the sand dunes and pine forests offer refuge to woodland species. Its wetlands provide a crucial stop for migrating birds, making Doñana an essential location on the migratory path between Europe and Africa. For those visiting during the right seasons, the park offers unrivaled opportunities to witness the spectacle of thousands of birds passing through or settling in the park.

Doñana is particularly well-known for its bird populations, and visitors can expect to see an incredible variety of species. One of the park's most famous residents is the Spanish imperial eagle, a rare and majestic bird of prey that has found a safe haven in the park's remote areas. Flamingos are another highlight, with large flocks often seen in the park's wetland areas. Herons, including the elegant purple heron and the striking black-crowned night heron, are also frequent visitors. The park is also home to a variety of waders, ducks, and other migratory species that make their way through the region in the spring and autumn.

The best times to visit Doñana are during the spring and autumn months, when the park's birdlife is at its most active. During these seasons, the park becomes a bustling hub for migrating birds. Spring sees a variety of species arriving to breed, while autumn is marked by an influx of birds making their way south for the winter. Visiting during these times offers the chance to witness the full spectacle of migration, with birdwatching opportunities at their peak. Summer can be hot, and bird activity slows down, while winter brings quieter days, though the park is still home to plenty of resident species.

To explore the park, the main entrance point is the visitor center in El Rocío, a picturesque village on the park's edge. From here, visitors can access the park's various areas and embark on guided tours. These tours are a great way to explore the park and increase your chances of spotting wildlife, as guides are knowledgeable about the area's flora and fauna. Guided tours typically range from €25 to €50, depending on the duration and type of tour. Tours can vary from walking excursions to safari-style trips in a 4x4 vehicle, which are ideal for covering larger areas of the park. These safaris usually last 3-4 hours and are a great way to gain insight into the park's biodiversity while comfortably observing wildlife.

For those looking to explore the park on their own, walking and cycling are great ways to experience the scenery up close. There are several well-marked trails throughout the park, some of which are suitable for cycling, while others lead through quieter areas perfect for a leisurely stroll. Keep in mind that some parts of the park are restricted to protect delicate ecosystems, so it's important to respect these boundaries and follow park guidelines. If you're not keen on walking or cycling, joining a guided safari is the most efficient way to explore the park, as it offers the opportunity to cover more ground and spot more wildlife in a shorter time.

For those planning to stay near the park, there are several accommodation options in the nearby towns of Almonte and Matalascañas. Almonte, just a short drive from the park, offers a variety of lodging options, including charming rural guesthouses and hotels with easy access to Doñana. Matalascañas, located along the coast, offers a range of seaside accommodations, perfect for those looking to combine birdwatching with a relaxing beach experience. Both towns offer ample dining options, where you can sample regional specialties, such as seafood and local Andalusian dishes, after a day of birdwatching.

Doñana National Park is a true gem for nature lovers, offering an unparalleled birdwatching experience in one of Europe's most ecologically significant areas. Whether you're observing flamingos in the wetlands, spotting rare eagles in the forest, or simply soaking in the beauty of this unique landscape, Doñana is a place where the wonders of nature are never far away. With its rich biodiversity, accessible tours, and stunning scenery, a visit to Doñana offers a chance to connect with the natural world in a profound way.

Costa del Sol

The Costa del Sol, Andalucía's Mediterranean coastline, is a  celebrated destination that draws millions of visitors each year with its golden beaches, luxurious resorts, and vibrant coastal towns. Stretching over 150 kilometers from Málaga to Gibraltar, this stretch of coast is a sun-drenched paradise known for its perfect weather, scenic beauty, and rich cultural history.

Málaga, the gateway to the Costa del Sol, is a bustling city with a mix of historic charm and modern appeal. The city's beaches, like Playa de la Malagueta, are some of the most popular along the coast. Located just a 10-minute walk from the city center, this busy beach is perfect for those who enjoy a lively atmosphere with plenty of beach bars and restaurants. You can rent a sunbed here for around €10-€15, or simply relax on the sand. The surrounding promenade offers stunning views of the sea, and you can easily pop into one of the many seaside restaurants for a fresh seafood meal.

Further along the coast, Marbella stands out for its luxury resorts, upscale dining, and vibrant nightlife. The city is famous for its glamorous marina, Puerto Banús, where you can see luxury yachts docked alongside high-end boutiques. Marbella's beaches are wide and sandy, with plenty of beach clubs where you can rent sunbeds or cabanas and enjoy the Mediterranean lifestyle in comfort. The cost of a sunbed at a beach club here typically ranges from €15 to €30, depending on the location and amenities provided. Marbella also offers a charming old town with cobblestone streets, whitewashed buildings, and traditional Andalusian architecture—perfect for a leisurely stroll after a day on the beach.

Estepona, another gem on the Costa del Sol, offers a more relaxed atmosphere compared to Marbella. With its flower-filled streets, the town exudes a tranquil, welcoming vibe. The beaches here are less crowded, making it an excellent choice for those seeking a quieter spot to unwind. Estepona's coastline is perfect for swimming, while its promenades lined with restaurants and cafes offer plenty of opportunities to savor local tapas and seafood dishes.

Further east, the town of Nerja is known for its striking cliffs and beautiful beaches, such as Playa Burriana. This beach is quieter than those in Málaga or Marbella, offering a more secluded spot for those looking to escape the crowds. Nerja's beaches are ideal for swimming and kayaking, and the nearby cliffs provide great spots for hiking, offering panoramic views of the coastline. The surrounding area is also home to the Sierras de Tejeda, Almijara, and Alhama Natural Park, a protected area perfect for outdoor enthusiasts looking to explore the mountainous terrain and diverse wildlife.

For those looking to explore beyond the beach, hiking along the cliffs or in the nearby nature reserves is highly recommended. The Sierras de Tejeda Natural Park offers a range of trails, from easy walks to more challenging routes, all with stunning views of the Mediterranean. The park is home to a rich variety of flora and fauna, making it a perfect destination for nature lovers.

Getting to the Costa del Sol is easy, with Málaga Airport (AGP) serving as the main international gateway. The airport is well-connected to towns along the coast by train and bus, with frequent services to Marbella, Estepona, and Nerja. Many of the coastal towns also have bus and train stations, making it convenient to hop between destinations. Renting a car is another good option for exploring the region at your own pace, especially if you want to visit some of the quieter, off-the-beaten-path beaches or venture into the surrounding countryside.

Accommodation options along the Costa del Sol range from boutique hotels to luxury beachfront resorts. In Málaga, you can find stylish boutique hotels in the historic center or near the beach, offering a mix of traditional charm and modern amenities. In Marbella, luxury resorts with all-inclusive packages and private beaches are the norm, while Estepona offers a range of more affordable, family-friendly options. For those seeking a truly serene getaway, there are also villas and small hotels nestled in the hills around Nerja, offering beautiful views and a peaceful atmosphere.

Cabo de Gata

Cabo de Gata-Níjar Natural Park, located in the southeastern corner of Spain, is a breathtaking coastal haven known for its untouched beauty and unique volcanic landscapes. This protected area, stretching over 30,000 hectares, is one of Spain's most

distinctive and unspoiled natural wonders. The park's striking geology—shaped by volcanic activity millions of years ago— creates a rugged, dramatic landscape of craggy cliffs, hidden coves, and pristine beaches that make it a true paradise for nature lovers.

One of the most remarkable features of Cabo de Gata is its volcanic terrain. The park is home to jagged hills, lava formations, and volcanic cones, which stand in stark contrast to the surrounding Mediterranean. The contrasts between the deep blues of the sea, the earthy browns of the cliffs, and the desert-like landscape make this area a photographer's dream. The park's geology also includes salt flats, caves, and fossilized dunes, all of which create a sense of otherworldliness, offering a serene environment for hiking, birdwatching, and more.

For outdoor enthusiasts, Cabo de Gata offers a wide range of activities that allow you to fully immerse yourself in its natural beauty. Hiking is one of the best ways to explore the park's diverse landscapes. There are numerous trails catering to all levels of experience, from easy coastal walks to more challenging hikes that take you to the park's highest points, offering panoramic views of the coast. One of the most popular hiking routes is the Sendero de los Genoveses, which takes you along scenic cliffs and sandy paths, leading to hidden beaches and providing sweeping views of the Mediterranean.

Snorkeling and kayaking are also fantastic ways to explore the park's crystal-clear waters and rich marine life. The beaches of Cabo de Gata are renowned for their untouched beauty, and the waters surrounding them are teeming with fish, colorful corals, and other marine creatures. The underwater landscape here is as dramatic as the land, with submerged volcanic rock formations and underwater caves that attract divers and snorkelers from around the world. Guided marine excursions are available for those who want to explore these waters with an expert, and prices typically range from €30 to €50 per person.

Cabo de Gata is also home to some of Spain's most beautiful and secluded beaches, two of the most famous being Playa de los Genoveses and Playa de Mónsul. Both beaches are located within the park and offer a perfect blend of relaxation, beauty, and isolation. Playa de los Genoveses is a wide, crescent-shaped beach surrounded by hills and dunes, making it ideal for a peaceful day by the sea. It's also a great spot for photography, especially at sunrise or sunset when the golden light illuminates the landscape. Playa de Mónsul, with its dramatic volcanic rock formations and turquoise waters, is equally stunning. Both beaches are relatively quiet, allowing visitors to enjoy the natural surroundings without the crowds often found at more tourist-heavy beaches.

The park's protected status makes it a haven for nature lovers and wildlife enthusiasts. With its diverse ecosystems, Cabo de Gata is home to many species of birds, including flamingos, herons, and other migratory birds that flock to the park's salt flats and wetlands. It's also a key habitat for marine life and desert flora, which thrive in the park's unique climate. The park's quiet, unspoiled environment offers a rare opportunity to connect with nature, making it an ideal destination for eco-tourism and outdoor exploration.

To reach Cabo de Gata, the nearest city is Almería, which is about a 30-minute drive from the park. Almería is well-connected by road and train, making it easy to access the park by car or public transport. Once in the park, it's best to explore by car, as some of the more remote beaches and hiking trails are off the beaten path. For those who prefer a guided experience, various companies offer hiking tours or marine excursions, providing expert guidance on the park's natural history and wildlife. These tours offer a deeper understanding of the park's ecosystems and help visitors discover hidden spots that might be missed otherwise.

For accommodation, there are plenty of eco-friendly options and rural tourism accommodations near the park. Many small hotels and guesthouses are nestled in the surrounding villages, offering comfortable stays with an emphasis on sustainability and respect for the natural environment. Staying in these rural accommodations allows visitors to experience the authentic Andalusian countryside while being close to the park's natural wonders.

Cabo de Gata-Níjar Natural Park is a must-visit destination for anyone looking to experience Spain's untamed beauty and unique landscapes. With its blend of dramatic landscapes, rich biodiversity, and tranquil environment, Cabo de Gata is a natural paradise that captures the essence of Andalucía's coastal charm.

The White Villages

The White Villages, or *Pueblos Blancos*, are a series of charming,  whitewashed towns scattered across the hills of Andalucía. These villages, perched on dramatic hillsides with stunning views of the surrounding valleys and mountains, offer visitors an authentic taste of rural Spain. Famous for their whitewashed buildings, winding streets, and centuries-old charm, these villages have been a beloved feature of the Andalusian landscape for centuries.

One of the most iconic of these villages is Ronda, renowned for its stunning location and dramatic history. Set atop a deep gorge, Ronda offers breathtaking views over the surrounding mountains and valleys. Its most famous landmark is the Puente Nuevo, a 18th-century bridge that spans the El Tajo gorge, offering a striking sight with a backdrop of rugged cliffs. Ronda's historic old town is filled with narrow streets, whitewashed buildings, and picturesque squares, making it a delightful place to explore on foot. The village is also known for its bullring, one of the oldest in Spain, and its role as a center of the Andalusian tradition of bullfighting.

Mijas, another popular village in the region, is located on the Costa del Sol but still retains a quaint, traditional charm. Perched high above the sea, Mijas offers panoramic views of the Mediterranean coastline. The village itself is a maze of cobblestone streets, whitewashed houses with colorful flowerpots, and small, family-run shops. Mijas is known for its calm atmosphere and its famous donkey taxis, which have become an iconic part of the village. It's a perfect spot for leisurely strolls, enjoying the views, and soaking up the local culture.

Múdejar, lesser-known but equally charming, is nestled in the hills and is a stunning example of Andalusian rural life. Its narrow streets and traditional white houses provide a glimpse into the simplicity and beauty of life in the Spanish countryside. Múdejar is also famous for its Moorish-inspired architecture, offering a quieter, more off-the-beaten-path experience compared to its more famous counterparts.

The tradition of whitewashing buildings in these villages dates back to ancient times. Originally, the practice of painting houses white was not just for aesthetic purposes but also practical. The intense summer heat in Andalucía made it essential to keep homes cool, and the reflective qualities of white paint helped to reduce the temperature inside the buildings. The bright white exteriors also reflected the region's abundant sunlight, creating a striking contrast against the surrounding natural landscapes.

Visiting the White Villages is a journey into the heart of Andalucía. The best way to explore these towns is by car, allowing you to take in the scenic drives through the hills and valleys. From Málaga, Ronda is about a 1.5-hour drive by bus, while Mijas is just a 30-minute drive from Marbella. The journey to these villages is as much a part of the experience as the destination itself, with winding roads offering sweeping views of the surrounding landscapes.

For those looking for a truly unforgettable scenic drive, a route through the Grazalema Natural Park is highly recommended. This park, located between the villages of Grazalema and Ubrique, is one of the most beautiful natural areas in Andalucía. The drive through the park offers breathtaking views of the Sierra de Grazalema mountains, dense forests, and deep ravines. If you're an avid hiker, this area is also known for its excellent hiking routes, offering trails for all levels of ability. The park is home to a variety of wildlife, including Spanish ibex, and its rich biodiversity makes it an excellent spot for nature lovers.

After a day of hiking or sightseeing, there's no better way to experience the Andalusian spirit than by enjoying a traditional meal at a local restaurant. The cuisine in these villages is rich with local flavors, and you can enjoy dishes like *rabo de toro* (oxtail stew) or *pisto* (a vegetable stew), often accompanied by a glass of local wine. A full meal in one of these rural restaurants will typically cost between €15 and €30, providing a great value for a taste of authentic Andalusian cuisine.

For accommodation, the White Villages offer a range of charming rural hotels and guesthouses. Many of these accommodations are family-run and provide a cozy, authentic experience. Staying in one of these rural guesthouses allows you to enjoy the tranquility of the countryside while still being within easy reach of the villages' attractions. These places often offer stunning views of the surrounding mountains and valleys, making your stay even more memorable.

The White Villages are an ideal destination for those looking to escape the hustle and bustle of the city and immerse themselves in the serene beauty of rural Andalucía. With their stunning landscapes, rich history, and welcoming atmosphere, the White Villages are a perfect representation of the enduring charm of this remarkable region.

Chapter 4: Culture, Festivals, and Traditions

Flamenco

Flamenco is not just a music and dance form; it's the soul of Andalucía, a cultural expression that pulses through the region's veins. Born from a fusion of diverse cultural influences, flamenco combines the passionate sounds of the Gypsies, the mystique of the Moors, the rhythms of Jewish traditions, and the deep roots of Andalusian folk music. This rich blend of cultures created a musical form that speaks to the heart and resonates with the very spirit of Andalucía.

At its core, flamenco consists of four main elements: the guitar, cante (singing), baile (dance), and palmas (hand clapping). Each element plays a crucial role in creating the unique rhythm and intensity that defines flamenco. The guitar provides the driving force, its strings plucked and strummed with skill and emotion, often playing complex, rapid patterns. The cante, or singing, is the heart of flamenco's soul—raw and heartfelt, with lyrics often exploring themes of love, loss, joy, and pain. The baile, or dance, is a powerful, expressive form of movement, with dancers using intricate footwork and graceful arm movements to convey the story of the music. Finally, palmas, the rhythmic hand clapping, adds another layer of percussive intensity to the performance, creating a vibrant, lively backdrop to the other elements.

To truly experience flamenco in its authentic form, there are several key cities in Andalucía where the art form thrives.

Seville is perhaps the most iconic of these cities. Known as the birthplace of flamenco, it offers numerous venues where you can enjoy the music and dance live. One of the best places to experience flamenco is Tablao El Arenal, an intimate venue in the heart of Seville, where talented dancers and musicians perform traditional flamenco shows. Tickets for a flamenco performance here typically range from €20 to €50, depending on the show and seating options. The passion of the performers in Seville is undeniable, and watching a flamenco show here feels like witnessing the very pulse of Andalucía.

Jerez de la Frontera is another city with a deep connection to flamenco. Known for its lively flamenco scene, Jerez has been home to many of the most influential flamenco artists. The city's flamenco festivals are a major draw, and many venues offer intimate performances that allow you to get up close to the action. The Flamenco Festival of Jerez, held annually in February or March, is one of the most prestigious flamenco events in Spain, attracting top-tier performers from around the world. Jerez is also the place to find flamenco schools where you can watch dancers perfecting their craft or take a class yourself.

Granada, with its Moorish history and enchanting atmosphere, is another excellent city for experiencing flamenco. The gypsy community of the Sacromonte neighborhood, set in the hills above the Alhambra, has long been a center for flamenco, and you can find performances in cave-like venues that add to the authentic experience. The intimate setting of these caves, where the acoustics amplify the intensity of the performance, makes it one of the best places in the world to watch flamenco.

For travelers keen to immerse themselves even deeper in flamenco, taking part in a workshop is a wonderful way to connect with this art form. Many cities, particularly Seville and Jerez, offer flamenco dance classes for beginners and enthusiasts alike. Group classes typically cost between €30 and €50 per person, depending on the duration and the level of instruction. These classes are a fun way to learn the basic steps and rhythms of flamenco and gain a greater appreciation for the dedication and skill required to perform. Some workshops even include a short performance at the end, allowing participants to show off their newly acquired moves.

If you're interested in buying flamenco attire or accessories, Seville and Jerez are great places to shop. In Seville, head to the historic district near the Plaza de España, where you'll find a variety of boutiques selling flamenco dresses (traje de flamenca), shawls (mantones), and castanets. These items make great souvenirs, and they're perfect for those who want to embrace the spirit of flamenco while enjoying the beauty of Andalucía. In Jerez, you can also find shops offering flamenco-inspired clothing and accessories, often with a more traditional flair.

The best time to experience flamenco in Andalucía is during the spring and fall. These seasons not only offer pleasant weather but also coincide with many of the region's flamenco festivals and events. Spring, in particular, is a great time to visit, as the cities come alive with celebrations like the Seville Fair and the Jerez Flamenco Festival, where flamenco is performed in public squares, bars, and theaters.

Flamenco is more than just a performance—it's an emotional journey that reflects the rich history, culture, and spirit of Andalucía. Whether you're watching a fiery dancer in Seville, enjoying a soulful singer in Jerez, or exploring the gypsy roots of flamenco in Granada, this art form offers a deep connection to the heart of Spain. For anyone seeking to truly understand the soul of Andalucía, flamenco is the key.

Semana Santa

Semana Santa, or Holy Week, is the most significant and emotional religious celebration in Andalucía, drawing thousands of visitors from around the world each year. This deeply Catholic tradition, which takes place in cities like Seville, Málaga, and Córdoba, is marked by dramatic processions that stretch through the streets, filled with passion, reverence, and striking displays of devotion. It is a week where the region's religious faith and cultural identity converge, creating an experience unlike any other.

The highlight of Semana Santa are the processions, which feature large wooden floats, known as *pasos*, depicting scenes from the Passion of Christ. These floats, often adorned with intricate carvings and religious images, are carried by *costaleros*—men who bear the weight of the *pasos* on their shoulders and necks. The floats are followed by *nazarenos*, individuals dressed in traditional robes and pointy hoods, often resembling the attire worn by medieval penitents. The processions wind through the streets, creating an intense atmosphere of solemnity and reflection. In cities like Seville, Málaga, and Córdoba, the processions can last for hours, with the floats passing through narrow streets lit only by candlelight, making the event feel both intimate and awe-inspiring.

Seville is one of the most famous cities to witness Semana Santa. The processions here are grand, elaborate, and emotionally charged, with some of the most iconic brotherhoods (hermandades) taking part. The atmosphere is palpable as crowds gather along the procession routes, many of whom have reserved seats for a better view. In Seville, reserved seats along the route can cost anywhere from €20 to €100, depending on the location and time of day. These prime spots offer a comfortable way to enjoy the processions, though it's just as common for spectators to stand along the route and join in the communal experience.

Semana Santa is a time of great reflection, and those attending should be mindful of the solemn nature of the event. Modest clothing is generally required, particularly if you plan to enter churches or religious buildings. For women, a simple dress or skirt with a covered neckline is appropriate, while men should wear long pants and avoid overly casual clothing. In many of the more religiously focused parts of the processions, locals and visitors alike respect the sacredness of the event by maintaining a reverent silence as the *pasos* pass by. This is not just a spectacle, but a deeply moving experience for the people of Andalucía, many of whom have participated in the processions for generations.

Semana Santa reflects Andalucía's profound Catholic traditions, but it also plays a huge cultural role in the region. In Seville, Málaga, and Córdoba, the processions are a point of pride for the locals. The craftsmanship involved in creating the *pasos* is often passed down through families, and the devotion shown by the *costaleros* and *nazarenos* is a testament to the deep-rooted faith that defines Andalucía. The event is as much a celebration of the region's identity as it is a religious observance, intertwining faith, tradition, and artistry in a way that few other festivals do.

The atmosphere of Semana Santa is unlike any other festival in Spain. The streets come alive with the sounds of drum beats, the solemn cries of the *saetas* (flamenco-style religious songs sung from balconies), and the clanging of chains carried by some participants. The streets are filled with both locals and tourists, but it's the local residents' participation in the processions that gives the event its true sense of community. In Málaga, for example, the crowds are not only watching but often singing along or offering prayers as the processions pass.

For those attending, it's important to plan ahead, as Semana Santa is one of the busiest travel times in Spain. Trains and buses to cities like Seville or Málaga are plentiful but can fill up quickly, so booking in advance is essential. The best vantage points for watching the processions are typically near the main squares or along the central streets where the floats tend to stop for rest periods. Some of the most iconic processions pass through Seville's Barrio Santa Cruz, while in Málaga, the processions through the historic center offer great opportunities for photographs and immersive experiences.

While watching the processions, it's also a great opportunity to enjoy the local food. Many street vendors set up near the processions, selling traditional Andalusian treats like *torrijas* (a type of French toast typically eaten during Semana Santa) and *churros* with hot chocolate. For a more substantial meal, local restaurants offer regional specialties such as *rabo de toro* (oxtail stew) and *pescaito frito* (fried fish), perfect for refueling between processions.

Feria de Abril

Feria de Abril (April Fair) is one of Seville's most beloved and exuberant celebrations, embodying the region's love for life, music, and dance. Held annually in late April, this vibrant festival is a kaleidoscope of colors, filled with flamenco dancing, horse parades, and private tents known as *casetas*, where friends and families gather to eat, drink, and enjoy the festivities. With its deep roots in Seville's culture, Feria de Abril offers a perfect glimpse into the heart of Andalusian traditions and the region's joyous spirit.

The origins of the Feria de Abril date back to 1846 when it was first held as a livestock fair. Over time, it evolved into a grand celebration of Andalusian culture, with an emphasis on music, dance, and social gatherings. Today, the fair takes place at the Real de la Feria, a large area near the Guadalquivir River, transformed into a colorful fairground filled with over a thousand *casetas*. These private tents, often owned by local families or social clubs, serve as gathering spots where people come together to enjoy food, drink, and music. The festive atmosphere is further amplified by the spectacular horse parades and the stunning flamenco performances that grace the event.

One of the most iconic moments of the Feria de Abril is the "alumbrao," which marks the official opening of the fair when the entire fairground is illuminated for the first time. This dazzling display of lights sets the stage for the next several days of celebration, as the fairgrounds come alive with music, dancing, and laughter. The night sky is filled with the glow of thousands of lights, creating a magical ambiance that continues throughout the festival.

The festival typically spans six days, starting on a Monday evening and ending the following Sunday. The first night is reserved for the *alumbrao*, a truly special event when the fair's lights are turned on, signaling the beginning of the celebrations. From there, the festival is filled with a range of activities, including horse-drawn carriage parades, flamenco dancing, and traditional Andalusian music. Visitors can watch elegantly dressed horse riders make their way through the fairgrounds, and at night, the sound of flamenco guitars and the rhythm of dancers' heels can be heard from the *casetas*. For those interested in more formal events, flamenco shows and concerts are held throughout the week, with ticket prices ranging from €15 to €40, depending on the performance.

When attending Feria de Abril, it's important to dress the part. Women traditionally wear *traje de flamenca*, the colorful, ruffled dresses that have become synonymous with the festival. These dresses, often adorned with polka dots and vibrant colors, are worn with accessories like flower crowns and shawls. Men typically wear traditional Andalusian outfits, often featuring a tailored jacket, pants, and a flat-brimmed hat. The festive dress adds to the charm and authenticity of the event, making it feel like you're stepping into a living, breathing tradition.

To fully experience the fair, it's essential to indulge in the local food and drink. Seville's tapas are legendary, and during the fair, you'll find some of the best examples at the *casetas*. Try traditional dishes like *jamón ibérico*, *tortilla española*, and *rebujito*, a refreshing drink made from manzanilla (sherry) and soda water, which is especially popular at the Feria. The fairgrounds are packed with food stalls and *casetas* offering local wines, sherries, and a variety of Andalusian snacks. Be prepared for the crowds, as the festival is a major event, and finding a table in a *caseta* can be tricky without a reservation. If you don't have access to a *caseta*, there are plenty of places around the fairgrounds where you can enjoy the food and soak in the atmosphere.

Getting to the Feria de Abril is relatively easy, as the fairgrounds are located just a short distance from Seville's city center. Visitors can take a bus or walk from the city center to the Real de la Feria, which is about 20 minutes from popular areas like Plaza de España. Taxis and horse-drawn carriages are also available for those who prefer a more traditional mode of transport. It's wise to plan your transport in advance, as the fair attracts a large number of people, and public transport can be crowded, particularly in the evenings.

Booking accommodation for Feria de Abril requires some advance planning, as Seville fills up quickly during this time. It's best to book your hotel or guesthouse well ahead of time, especially if you want to stay near the fairgrounds. Many visitors opt to stay in the city center, which offers easy access to the festival and is home to a wide range of accommodations, from boutique hotels to more luxurious options.

To make the most of Feria de Abril, try to visit during the week's prime moments—typically from Thursday to Saturday—when the fair is at its liveliest. However, it's important to keep in mind that the Feria is as much about the local community as it is about the visitors, so embrace the cultural experience, join in the dancing, and enjoy the vibrant atmosphere that makes Seville's April Fair one of the most exciting celebrations in Spain.

Local Craftsmanship

Pottery is one of the most well-known crafts in Andalucía, and towns like Úbeda and Mijas are particularly famous for their hand-painted ceramics and tiles. The ceramic tradition here dates back centuries, with vibrant, bold colors and intricate designs inspired by Andalusia's Moorish past. In Mijas, you can find a range of beautifully painted ceramics, from colorful plates and bowls to ornate tiles perfect for decorating your home. Prices for handcrafted pottery typically range from €10 to €100, depending on the item and its size. For a more personal touch, many shops offer the opportunity to watch artisans at work, allowing visitors to appreciate the skill and patience involved in creating each piece. Úbeda, known for its Renaissance architecture, also boasts a long-standing ceramic tradition, with local workshops showcasing pieces that reflect the region's historical influences.

Another significant craft in Andalucía is leatherwork, particularly in Córdoba, a city famous for its fine craftsmanship. Córdoba's leather artisans are known for their beautifully hand-stitched bags, belts, shoes, and other accessories. These products, often made from high-quality leather, are crafted with incredible attention to detail and can be found in many small shops around the city. Leatherwork in Córdoba has been a part of its heritage for centuries, with techniques passed down through generations. Prices for leather goods vary, but you can expect to pay between €30 and €100 for high-quality, handmade leather bags or belts. Visiting the artisan workshops in Córdoba is a great way to see the process firsthand, with many shops offering demonstrations or tours that explain the history and techniques behind this craft.

For those looking to immerse themselves in the craftsmanship of Andalucía, visiting local markets is a must. Seville's Mercado de Artesanía is open year-round and offers a wide array of handmade products, from ceramics and leather goods to textiles and jewelry. The market is a perfect place to explore and purchase authentic products directly from the artisans themselves, giving you a chance to speak with the creators and learn more about the techniques involved in their work. In Ronda, there are monthly craft markets where visitors can find handmade goods like wood carvings, woven textiles, and pottery. These markets are a great way to discover local craftsmanship while enjoying the picturesque setting of Ronda.

For those interested in learning the crafts firsthand, Andalucía offers plenty of opportunities to participate in workshops. In Mijas, visitors can take ceramic workshops, where they learn how to shape and paint their own pottery. Prices for these workshops range from €25 to €50 for a half-day session, and they provide a fun and educational experience, allowing you to create a personal souvenir while gaining insight into the region's rich ceramic tradition. In Córdoba, leatherworking classes are available, where you can learn how to craft your own leather items such as belts or wallets. These workshops, also priced between €25 and €50 for a half-day session, offer a unique opportunity to connect with the craft and take home a handmade product you've created yourself.

Incorporating these artisanal experiences into your travel itinerary is a wonderful way to dive deeper into the local culture of Andalucía. By visiting workshops or markets, you can appreciate the artistry and dedication that goes into the region's handicrafts, and perhaps even bring home a piece of Andalucía's rich artistic tradition.

Culinary Traditions

Andalucía, a region known for its rich history and culture, offers a culinary heritage as vibrant and diverse as its landscapes. The foundation of Andalusian cuisine lies in its most famous tradition: tapas. These small, flavorful dishes are a perfect representation of the region's approach to dining—simple yet packed with flavor. But tapas are just the beginning.

The origin of tapas is a bit murky, but it is believed that the tradition began in the southern part of Spain when bartenders would serve small portions of food atop drinks to keep the flies away. Over time, tapas evolved into a delightful social experience, with bars and restaurants offering a variety of bite-sized dishes to enjoy with friends or family. Tapas can range from the simplest olives or cheese to more complex creations like fried fish, meats, and stews. In Andalucía, a typical tapas meal will cost between €10 and €20 per person, depending on where you are dining. This makes tapas an affordable and accessible way to sample a variety of Andalusian flavors in one sitting.

Among the most iconic tapas is jamón ibérico, a dry-cured Spanish ham that is considered one of the best in the world. The rich, savory flavor of jamón ibérico is the result of an intricate curing process that takes years to complete, and it is a must-try in Andalucía. Another beloved dish is pescaíto frito, which consists of small, lightly battered and fried fish, typically served as a tapa in coastal towns like Málaga and Cádiz. Whether it's anchovies, squid, or whitebait, pescaíto frito is a true reflection of the region's coastal cuisine. And when the summer heat hits, there's nothing more refreshing than a bowl of gazpacho, a cold tomato-based soup mixed with cucumbers, peppers, and a generous amount of olive oil. Gazpacho is a staple in Andalucía, especially during the scorching summer months, offering a cooling and light meal.

Speaking of olive oil, Andalucía is the birthplace of one of the world's finest oils. The region is responsible for producing around 50% of Spain's olive oil, with the area around Baena, in the Córdoba province, being particularly famous for its high-quality extra virgin olive oil. Olive oil is a cornerstone of Andalusian cuisine, used not only in cooking but also as a condiment for nearly every dish. From drizzling it over fresh salads to using it in sauces and stews, olive oil is integral to the flavors of the region. The process of olive harvesting is a labor-intensive tradition, passed down for generations. Olive trees, some of which are centuries old, are carefully tended to, with olives handpicked during harvest season.

For visitors looking to delve deeper into the world of olive oil, there are several excellent places to visit. In the Montes de Toledo area, there are numerous olive oil farms offering tours and tastings, where you can learn about the history, production, and uses of olive oil. The Olive Oil Museum in Baena also offers an immersive experience, with tasting tours ranging from €5 to €15. These tours give visitors a hands-on understanding of how olive oil is made, along with the chance to sample various oils and learn how to differentiate between high-quality oils based on flavor and aroma.

Beyond tapas, Andalucía boasts other regional dishes that showcase the diversity of its cuisine. One such dish is salmorejo, a thicker, richer version of gazpacho made with tomatoes, bread, and olive oil. It's often served topped with hard-boiled eggs and jamón ibérico. You'll find this dish most often in Córdoba, where it's prepared with the freshest local ingredients and served as a comforting, hearty meal. For the best experience, head to a traditional family-run restaurant or a local market, where these dishes are made with time-honored recipes and served with a generous helping of local hospitality.

For those looking to gain a deeper understanding of Andalusian cuisine, taking part in a food tour or cooking class is an excellent way to explore the region's culinary traditions. Many cities, including Seville, Córdoba, and Granada, offer food tours that take you through local markets, tapas bars, and hidden gems, allowing you to taste the best of Andalusian fare while learning about the region's food culture. Cooking classes are also widely available, offering visitors the opportunity to learn how to prepare Andalusian dishes themselves. Classes typically range from €40 to €80 per person for a half-day workshop, where you can get hands-on experience making tapas, paella, or even a full-course Andalusian meal.

Chapter 5: Exploring Andalucian History and Heritage

The Alhambra

The Alhambra in Granada stands as one of the most iconic and breathtaking examples of Moorish architecture, drawing visitors from all over the world to admire its intricate beauty and historical significance. This UNESCO World Heritage site, originally built as a fortress in the 13th century, was later transformed into a royal palace by the Nasrid dynasty. Today, it is not only a symbol of Islamic art and architecture but also a testament to the cultural exchange between different civilizations in medieval Spain.

The origins of the Alhambra trace back to 1238, when Muhammad I of Granada, the founder of the Nasrid dynasty, began constructing what was initially intended to be a defensive stronghold. Over the centuries, successive rulers expanded the site, transforming it into a grand palace complex. The name "Alhambra" comes from the Arabic word "al-ḥamrā," meaning "the red one," likely referencing the reddish hue of the fortress walls that are particularly striking at sunset. As the Alhambra evolved from a military fortification to the residence of the Nasrid sultans, it became a center of culture, art, and power, with its stunning gardens, courtyards, and elaborate decorations.

The architectural beauty of the Alhambra is unparalleled. The intricate stucco work that adorns the walls and ceilings is a hallmark of Moorish craftsmanship, showcasing geometric patterns and delicate floral motifs that seem to shimmer in the light. The famous Hall of the Ambassadors, where the sultans held court, is a perfect example of this ornate decoration, with its richly detailed ceilings and breathtaking views across the city of Granada. The Alhambra's courtyards, such as the Patio de los Leones, are equally impressive, with their symmetry and serene water features. The rhythmic sound of fountains flowing through these peaceful courtyards creates an atmosphere of tranquility, inviting visitors to pause and reflect.

The Alhambra is also known for its lush gardens, most notably the Generalife Gardens, which are located just a short distance from the palace complex. Originally designed as a summer retreat for the sultans, the Generalife is a masterpiece of Islamic garden design, featuring flowing water, vibrant flowers, and shady pathways. The panoramic views of Granada and the surrounding Sierra Nevada mountains from the gardens are simply breathtaking, making it a must-visit spot during any trip to the Alhambra.

Visiting the Alhambra is an experience that should be planned in advance, especially during peak tourist season. Entry to the Alhambra ranges from €14 to €20, depending on the time of year and the type of ticket purchased. Because of its popularity, it's highly recommended to book your tickets in advance to avoid disappointment, as they often sell out, particularly during the spring and summer months. The best times to visit are either early in the morning or later in the afternoon when the crowds tend to thin out. Arriving at these times allows you to experience the Alhambra in a more serene atmosphere, with the golden light of the early morning or the soft hues of sunset adding to its magic.

While you can explore the Alhambra on your own, taking a guided tour can significantly enhance your experience by providing deeper historical context and insights into the site's art and architecture. Guided tours typically cost between €30 and €60 per person, depending on the length of the tour and the level of expertise of the guide. A knowledgeable guide can help you better understand the significance of the various features of the Alhambra, such as the symbolism of the intricate tilework or the role of the water features in Islamic garden design. Many tours also include visits to the Generalife Gardens, offering a comprehensive look at the entire Alhambra complex.

Reaching the Alhambra from Granada's city center is relatively easy. The most common options are by bus or taxi, both of which take about 15 minutes. There are frequent buses that run from the city center to the Alhambra, or you can take a taxi for a more direct and comfortable journey. Walking to the Alhambra is also an option, though it is a bit of a climb up the hill, and it may take around 30 minutes from the center.

For accommodations, there are a variety of options nearby, ranging from charming boutique hotels to more luxurious establishments. Staying near the Alhambra or in Granada's historic center gives you easy access to the palace and other attractions, such as the Albayzín neighborhood, with its narrow winding streets and whitewashed houses that evoke the region's Moorish past.

The Alhambra is much more than a mere tourist attraction—it is a symbol of the cultural richness and historical depth of Spain.

Its architecture, gardens, and views are a window into a time when this remarkable fortress and palace was at the center of Islamic Spain.

Mezquita of Cordoba

The Mezquita of Córdoba stands as one of Spain's most extraordinary architectural feats, a breathtaking monument that seamlessly blends Islamic and Christian influences. Initially constructed in the 8th century as a mosque, it was later transformed into a cathedral in the 13th century, creating a unique cultural and religious landmark. The Mezquita is not just a place of worship; it is a striking symbol of Córdoba's rich history and its role as a cultural crossroads between different civilizations.

The mosque's construction began in 785, under the reign of the Umayyad caliph, Abd al-Rahman I. Over the next several centuries, successive rulers expanded the building, transforming it into one of the largest mosques in the world at the time. The most iconic feature of the Mezquita is its mesmerizing red-and-white arches, which are made from alternating red brick and white stone. These arches create a sense of infinite space, with the hundreds of columns in the vast prayer hall seemingly stretching endlessly. Walking through the prayer hall is like entering another world, where light filters through delicate windows, casting shadows on the intricate geometric designs of the floor and ceiling.

One of the most awe-inspiring parts of the mosque is the mihrab, the prayer niche that points toward Mecca. The mihrab is a stunning example of Islamic artistry, with its delicate mosaic tiles and golden accents creating a luminous focal point in the building. The vast, serene space of the Mezquita invites quiet reflection, and the harmonious blend of Islamic architectural elegance and Christian modifications throughout the centuries tells the story of Córdoba's complex cultural heritage.

In the 13th century, after the Christian reconquest of Córdoba, the mosque was converted into a cathedral. The transformation was not just a change in function but also in form, as Christian elements were integrated into the structure. The most notable of these is the addition of a Renaissance nave and the placement of a Baroque altar in the center of the building. While the fusion of styles might seem incongruous at first glance, it adds to the Mezquita's unique character and serves as a testament to the layered history of this remarkable site.

Visiting the Mezquita is a deeply moving experience, and the cost of entry is around €10, making it an affordable way to experience one of the most culturally significant monuments in Spain. The Mezquita is conveniently located in the heart of Córdoba, just a 10-minute walk from the train station, making it easy to reach from the city center. To fully appreciate the history and significance of this architectural masterpiece, it's highly recommended to take a guided tour. Tours typically cost between €15 and €25 per person, and they provide invaluable context on the Mezquita's evolution, the cultural influences that shaped it, and the fascinating interplay of Islamic and Christian elements.

In addition to the main prayer hall and mihrab, visitors can explore the adjacent Courtyard of Orange Trees, a tranquil space filled with fragrant citrus trees. This beautiful courtyard offers a peaceful escape from the crowds and provides a lovely view of the Mezquita's exterior. The bell tower, which was originally the mosque's minaret, also offers stunning views of the city. The climb to the top of the tower is well worth the effort, as it provides panoramic views of Córdoba's rooftops, the Guadalquivir River, and the surrounding countryside.

For those hoping to avoid large crowds, the best times to visit the Mezquita are early in the morning or late in the afternoon, especially on weekdays. Córdoba is a popular tourist destination, so arriving early allows you to experience the grandeur of the Mezquita in relative peace before the crowds arrive. If you're visiting during peak tourist season, be sure to book tickets in advance, as the site often fills up quickly.

The Mezquita of Córdoba is more than just an architectural wonder; it is a living testament to the city's long and rich history. It encapsulates the fusion of cultures, religions, and artistic traditions that have shaped Córdoba over the centuries.

The Roman Ruins of Italica

Just a short journey outside of Seville lies Itálica, an ancient Roman city that offers a fascinating glimpse into the past. Founded in the 3rd century BCE, Itálica was once a thriving Roman settlement, notable not only for its grandeur but also as the birthplace of two Roman emperors, Trajan and Hadrian. Today, the well-preserved ruins of Itálica allow visitors to step back in time and explore one of the most important archaeological sites in Andalucía.

One of the most striking features of Itálica is its grand amphitheater, which once held up to 25,000 spectators. This impressive structure is one of the best-preserved Roman amphitheaters in Spain and gives a vivid sense of the scale and importance of public entertainment in ancient Roman life. The amphitheater, used for gladiatorial games and other spectacles, offers a glimpse into the world of ancient Rome's most popular pastimes. Visitors can walk along the perimeter of the arena and imagine the crowds of Romans cheering for their favorite gladiators or watching staged naval battles in the flooded arena. The grandeur of the amphitheater is a testament to the engineering and architectural achievements of the Romans.

As you wander through the site, you'll also find remnants of the city's intricate residential areas. The ancient houses of Itálica, particularly those located near the center of the city, showcase beautiful mosaics that have survived centuries of wear. These mosaics, often depicting scenes from mythology, daily life, and nature, are remarkably detailed and provide a unique insight into the artistic and cultural practices of the time. The intricate designs in these homes highlight the wealth and sophistication of the city's residents.

In addition to the amphitheater and the mosaics, another significant part of the ruins is the House of the Gladiators. This well-preserved structure was likely the residence of some of the fighters who performed in the amphitheater. The house features a courtyard and rooms adorned with vibrant mosaics, offering a glimpse into the daily lives of the people who once lived there. The mix of luxury and function in these homes is a striking reminder of the Roman Empire's ability to blend artistic beauty with practical design.

Itálica is easily accessible from Seville, with a 20-minute bus ride from the city center making it a convenient day trip. The cost of entry to the site is very affordable, typically around €1.50, making it an excellent option for those wanting to explore Roman history on a budget. Once at the site, it's easy to navigate the expansive ruins, and most visitors head straight for the amphitheater, the mosaics, and the House of the Gladiators, which are the most famous and well-preserved parts of the city.

For those looking to deepen their understanding of the site, a guided tour is highly recommended. A guided tour, which typically costs between €10 and €15, provides valuable historical context and will enhance your experience of exploring Itálica. The guides offer fascinating insights into the history of the Roman Empire in Andalucía, shedding light on the importance of Itálica as a military and cultural center in Roman Spain.

The best time to visit Itálica is during the spring and autumn months when the weather is milder, and the site is less crowded. The ruins are also stunning at sunrise and sunset, when the soft light casts long shadows across the stones, enhancing the atmosphere of the ancient city.

The Legacy of Andalucian Kings and Queens

The Almohad dynasty, one of the most powerful Muslim dynasties to rule over Andalusia, was responsible for some of the region's most iconic architectural achievements. The Giralda in Seville, originally built as a minaret during the reign of the Almohads, is perhaps the most famous landmark from this period. Today, the Giralda remains a symbol of Seville, standing tall above the city with its intricate geometric patterns and elegant proportions. The Almohads also left their mark on the Alcázar of Seville, a stunning palace complex that showcases the dynasty's unique blend of Islamic, Gothic, and Renaissance architecture. The Alcázar's lush gardens, ornate tile work, and tranquil courtyards still offer a glimpse into the luxury and sophistication of the royal court during the Almohad period. Visiting the Royal Alcázar, with its entry fee of €14, is an opportunity to immerse yourself in the history of one of the most influential Muslim dynasties to rule Andalucía.

Another defining period in Andalucía's royal history is the Nasrid dynasty, whose rule culminated in the creation of the Alhambra in Granada. The Alhambra, a masterpiece of Islamic architecture, is not only a symbol of the Nasrid dynasty's artistic achievements but also a testament to their power and wealth. The palace's delicate stucco work, lush gardens, and serene courtyards evoke the splendor of the Nasrid court. The Alhambra's intricate design, which blends geometry with nature, reflects the Nasrid kings' deep appreciation for beauty and their sophisticated understanding of architecture. Visiting the Alhambra offers a glimpse into the golden age of Islamic Spain, where art, science, and culture flourished under the rule of the Nasrids.

In addition to the Muslim monarchs, Christian kings and queens played a vital role in shaping the history of Andalucía, particularly during the Christian Reconquista. King Ferdinand III of Castile, known as Saint Ferdinand, was one of the most influential figures in the Christian reclaiming of the Iberian Peninsula. His victory over the Moors in 1236 led to the capture of Seville, marking a key turning point in the Reconquista.

Ferdinand's reign left a lasting legacy, not just in military victories but also in the consolidation of Christian rule in Andalucía. His tomb, alongside that of his wife, Queen Beatrice, can be found in the Seville Cathedral, a testament to their pivotal role in the region's history. The entry fee to the cathedral is €9, which includes access to the tombs of Ferdinand and Isabella, two of Spain's most renowned monarchs.

Queen Isabella, alongside her husband Ferdinand, is perhaps best remembered for her role in the Spanish exploration and the discovery of the New World. Their reign marked the completion of the Reconquista and the unification of Spain, setting the stage for Spain's later global empire. Isabella's patronage of Christopher Columbus' voyages led to the opening of the Americas, forever changing the course of history. The influence of Isabella and Ferdinand extended beyond Spain, shaping the world as we know it today. The tombs of both monarchs in Seville are a poignant reminder of their contributions to Spanish and global history.

To truly understand the power dynamics of medieval Andalucía, a visit to these royal sites is essential. The Alcázar in Seville and the tombs of Ferdinand and Isabella provide a fascinating insight into the lives of the monarchs who shaped the region's cultural and political landscape. The Alhambra, with its delicate beauty and grandeur, speaks to the lasting legacy of the Nasrids and the influence of Islamic rule in Andalucía.

These historical landmarks, with their mix of Islamic and Christian influences, offer a unique window into the complex power struggles, cultural exchanges, and artistic achievements that defined medieval Andalucía..

Castles and Fortresses

One of the most iconic castles in Andalucía is the Alcázar of Jerez, located in the historic town of Jerez de la Frontera. Originally built as a fortress by the Moors in the 11th century, the Alcázar is a stunning example of Islamic architecture mixed with later Christian additions. The castle is surrounded by impressive defensive walls, towers, and battlements, with intricate arches and courtyards showcasing Moorish craftsmanship. One of its most remarkable features is the Torre del Homenaje (Homage Tower), which offers spectacular views of Jerez and the surrounding countryside. Entry to the Alcázar costs around €8, making it an affordable way to explore both the town's history and its scenic beauty. The best time to visit for photography is in the early morning or late afternoon when the warm light casts shadows across the ancient stone walls and enhances the texture of the fortifications.

In Málaga, the Castle of Gibralfaro stands proudly above the city, offering sweeping views of the Mediterranean coastline. Built in the 14th century by the Nasrid dynasty to defend the nearby Alcazaba, the Gibralfaro Castle played a significant role in military defense during the Reconquista. The castle's imposing structure, with its thick defensive walls and watchtowers, tells the story of Málaga's strategic importance during the Middle Ages. A visit to the castle costs around €4 to €5, and it's well worth the price for the panoramic vistas over the city, the sea, and the nearby mountains. For the best views and the most striking photographs, it's advisable to visit just before sunset, when the golden light makes the city's landscape glow and casts long shadows over the battlements.

Another impressive fortress is the Castle of Almodóvar del Río, located just outside Córdoba. This castle is a striking example of a medieval stronghold, with a history that dates back to the 8th century. Although much of it was rebuilt in the 15th century, the castle retains its original charm, with towering walls, a drawbridge, and a number of well-preserved towers. The Castle of Almodóvar played a key role during the Reconquista, and it's one of the best-preserved castles in the region. The cost of entry is around €8, and visitors can explore its vast courtyards, climb to the top of the towers for incredible views, and wander through its meticulously restored interiors. The castle's dramatic location, perched atop a hill overlooking the Guadalquivir River, makes it an ideal spot for photography, particularly at sunrise or sunset when the surrounding countryside is bathed in warm light.

These castles are not just architectural wonders; they are also historically significant. They served as fortresses during the centuries-long struggle between Muslims and Christians, playing key roles in both the defense and conquest of Andalusia. The Alcázar of Jerez, for example, was a strategic military base during the Christian Reconquista, and the Castle of Gibralfaro was part of Málaga's defense during the siege by the Catholic Monarchs. These fortifications are a testament to the region's military history, and visiting them allows you to walk in the footsteps of medieval soldiers and rulers.

When visiting these castles, it's also worth exploring the nearby towns. Ronda, for instance, is home to the dramatic Puente Nuevo bridge, which spans a deep gorge and connects the old and new parts of the town. The views from the bridge are breathtaking, offering a dramatic vista of the surrounding mountains and valley below. Ronda's historical charm, with its mix of Moorish and Christian architecture, complements the town's spectacular natural surroundings. It's a great place to spend a day after visiting the nearby Castle of Almodóvar del Río.

Getting to these castles is relatively straightforward. Most are easily accessible by car, and there are also bus services that connect the sites with nearby towns and cities. For a more immersive experience, guided tours are available, ranging in price from €10 to €20, which often include transport and a deeper historical context. When planning your visit, it's important to check opening hours and ticket availability, particularly during peak tourist seasons, as these sites can attract large crowds.

For accommodations, there are numerous charming hotels and guesthouses near these historical landmarks, ranging from rural retreats to more luxurious options. Staying in a nearby town allows you to immerse yourself in the local culture and enjoy Andalusian hospitality after a day of exploring the castles and fortresses.

Chapter 6: Outdoor Adventures in Andalucia

Hiking in the Sierra de Grazalema

The Sierra de Grazalema Natural Park is one of Andalucía's most stunning and biodiverse landscapes, a true haven for outdoor enthusiasts and nature lovers alike. Nestled between the provinces of Cádiz and Málaga, this park is famous for its lush greenery, dramatic limestone cliffs, dense forests, and serene rivers. The park's varied terrain offers a range of hiking trails suitable for all levels, from easy walks to more challenging routes that take you deep into the heart of the mountains.

One of the most popular hikes in the park is the Puerto de las Palomas, a scenic route that takes you along winding paths, offering breathtaking views of the surrounding valleys, cliffs, and the iconic peaks of the Sierra. The hike itself is moderate in difficulty, with some steep sections, but the effort is well worth it for the stunning panoramic vistas you'll enjoy along the way. From the summit, the view stretches for miles, with the rugged mountains providing a stark contrast to the lush green valleys below. The best times to hike this route are early in the morning or late in the afternoon when the light is soft, casting long shadows across the landscape and enhancing the dramatic scenery.

For those interested in a combination of nature and history, the Cueva de la Pileta is a must-see. This cave, known for its prehistoric cave paintings, offers a fascinating glimpse into the past. The paintings inside the cave, some of which date back over 20,000 years, depict animals, human figures, and symbols, providing a rare and valuable insight into the lives of ancient peoples who once roamed this region. The hike to the cave itself is relatively easy, but visitors should check for specific opening times, as access to the cave is sometimes restricted to guided tours. A visit here is an opportunity to explore both the beauty of the landscape and the cultural heritage of the park.

Entering the park itself is free, allowing you to immerse yourself in its natural beauty without any entrance fees. The park is easily accessible from Ronda, which is about a 45-minute drive away. From the city, it's a straightforward journey by car, and the drive through the Andalusian countryside is just as picturesque as the hikes themselves. The winding roads offer stunning views of the mountains, making the journey as much a part of the experience as the hike.

When preparing for a hike in the Sierra de Grazalema, it's important to pack appropriately. Sturdy hiking shoes are a must, as the trails can be uneven and rocky, especially in the more rugged areas of the park. Since the park is home to both sunny and shaded areas, it's essential to bring water to stay hydrated, as well as sunscreen and a hat to protect yourself from the sun. If you're hiking for a full day, it's also a good idea to pack snacks or a packed lunch to enjoy during your break, allowing you to fully immerse yourself in the natural beauty of the surroundings without rushing.

After a rewarding hike, be sure to visit the charming village of Grazalema. Known for its whitewashed buildings and narrow, cobblestone streets, the village offers a serene escape from the more strenuous outdoor activities. Grazalema is also a great place to explore local shops that sell regional products, from handmade leather goods to traditional cheese made from the milk of local goats. The village is known for its artisanal products, and strolling through its streets is a perfect way to unwind after a day of hiking.

For those who prefer a more guided experience, several local tour companies offer hiking excursions in the Sierra de Grazalema. These guided tours typically cost between €25 and €50 per person for a full-day hike, depending on the group size and the route. A local guide can provide valuable insight into the region's flora, fauna, and history, making the hike even more enriching. Whether you choose to go solo or join a group, a hike in the Sierra de Grazalema is an unforgettable way to experience the natural beauty and cultural heritage of one of Andalucía's most scenic areas.

Cycling Through Andalucia's Countryside

One of the most popular and accessible cycling routes in Andalucía is the Via Verde de la Sierra, a 36-kilometer-long path that takes cyclists through some of the region's most beautiful countryside. Originally a railway line, the route has been converted into a well-maintained, car-free cycling trail that passes through forests, valleys, and quaint villages. The route's gentle incline makes it suitable for cyclists of all levels, whether you're a beginner or a seasoned rider. Along the way, cyclists can enjoy scenic views of the Andalusian countryside, making it an ideal ride for those who want to take their time and soak in the surroundings.

For those looking for more challenging terrain, the Sierra de Aracena offers a more rugged and demanding cycling experience. The region's mountain trails provide a mix of steep ascents and thrilling descents, perfect for experienced cyclists seeking adventure. The route takes you through dense forests, past rolling hills, and offers spectacular panoramic views of the surrounding area. The terrain here can be more demanding, with some routes offering technical challenges that require a certain level of fitness and skill. But the reward is well worth the effort—breathtaking views and the satisfaction of conquering the rugged peaks of the Sierra de Aracena.

Cycling in Andalucía is made even easier with the abundance of bike rental shops in popular towns like Ronda and Córdoba. Bike rentals typically cost between €15 and €25 per day, depending on the type of bike and the rental shop. For those who prefer a more structured experience, local cycling tours are available in many regions. These tours, which generally cost between €50 and €80 per person, offer a guided cycling experience that includes route planning, bike rental, and insights into the local history and culture. Whether you're cycling along the scenic routes of Ronda or exploring the vineyards near Jerez, a guided tour is a great way to see the countryside without worrying about logistics.

When preparing for a cycling tour or a day of cycling through the Andalusian countryside, there are a few essential items to bring. A helmet is a must, ensuring both safety and comfort. The sun in Andalucía can be intense, so sunscreen is essential, especially for longer rides. A water bottle is also key, as staying hydrated is crucial during the hot summer months. Additionally, it's a good idea to bring lightweight, breathable clothing to stay cool during your ride, as well as a small backpack or saddlebag to carry any necessary supplies, such as snacks or a light jacket for cooler evenings.

Some of the most scenic spots for cycling in Andalucía include Cazalla de la Sierra, a small town nestled in the heart of the Sierra Norte de Sevilla. The town is surrounded by lush forests and rolling hills, making it an excellent starting point for a bike ride through the natural park. The routes here are relatively gentle, perfect for leisurely cycling, and they offer stunning views of the region's distinctive countryside. Málaga, with its combination of coastal roads and inland hills, is another fantastic cycling destination. The routes around Málaga offer cyclists the opportunity to explore both the Mediterranean coastline and the more mountainous inland areas. From the city, you can head out to picturesque villages or tackle the hills for more challenging rides with views of the sparkling sea below.

For those staying in larger cities like Seville or Granada, there are also great opportunities for shorter, city-based rides. Seville, for example, has a network of dedicated cycling lanes, making it easy to explore the city's historic center and beautiful parks by bike. Similarly, in Granada, cycling through the Albayzín district or around the Sierra Nevada foothills can provide a mix of urban and natural landscapes.

Rock Climbing in El Chorro

El Chorro, nestled in the stunning landscape of Málaga province, has long been one of Europe's most sought-after rock climbing destinations. Known for its dramatic cliffs, challenging routes, and breathtaking views, it's a place where climbers of all levels—from beginners to experts—come to test their skills against the backdrop of the rugged Andalusian countryside. With over 500 climbing routes to explore, El Chorro offers something for everyone, whether you're scaling vertical rock faces or simply taking in the scenery from a ledge high above the Guadalhorce River.

One of the most iconic spots for rock climbing in El Chorro is the Desfiladero de los Gaitanes, a spectacular gorge carved by the Guadalhorce River. The towering limestone cliffs that line the gorge are not just beautiful—they also offer some of the most challenging climbing in the region. Climbers can scale dramatic rock faces that rise sharply from the river, often with steep drops that provide a thrilling sense of exposure. The routes here vary in difficulty, making it an ideal spot for climbers of all abilities. For those seeking an adrenaline rush, the sense of climbing above a deep gorge, with the river far below, is an experience unlike any other.

In addition to the climbing routes, the Caminito del Rey—an accessible cliff-side walkway—is another highlight of the area. Originally built in the early 20th century for workers, this narrow path clings to the side of the gorge, offering incredible views of the valley and the surrounding mountains. While it's not a climbing route, it's a popular activity for those who want to experience the awe-inspiring landscapes of El Chorro without scaling the cliffs. For a fee of €10, visitors can walk the 7.7-kilometer route, which takes them across narrow wooden walkways, suspended high above the river. The Caminito del Rey is particularly stunning at sunrise or sunset when the cliffs are bathed in soft light, casting long shadows over the gorge.

Getting to El Chorro is relatively easy, especially if you're based in Málaga. The area is just about an hour's drive from the city, making it a convenient day trip for those staying in the coastal city. Once you arrive in El Chorro, you'll find a variety of climbing routes and walking trails to explore, but the area's true allure is in the way it combines both challenging climbs and spectacular views. For those who don't have their own gear or need guidance, several local climbing schools offer equipment rentals and guided climbing experiences. These tours typically range from €40 to €70 per person for a half-day, depending on the type of climbing experience you want—whether it's top-rope, sport, or trad climbing.

For newcomers to the sport, these guided tours are an excellent way to get a feel for climbing in El Chorro. Local climbing instructors are experienced and can tailor the session to your skill level, offering tips and encouragement as you tackle the routes. The instructors also provide all necessary equipment, from harnesses to ropes, so you can focus solely on the climb itself. For more seasoned climbers, multi-day climbing trips are available that allow you to explore the full range of routes the area has to offer, including the most challenging and remote climbs.

If you're not into climbing but still want to immerse yourself in El Chorro's stunning landscapes, the surrounding Sierra de las Nieves offers excellent hiking opportunities. The region is part of a natural park known for its biodiversity and rugged beauty. Trails through the Sierra de las Nieves allow hikers to explore the natural terrain at a more leisurely pace while enjoying the panoramic views that make this part of Andalucía so special. The park is home to a variety of wildlife, including mountain goats and wild boar, and offers peaceful surroundings for those looking to connect with nature away from the more popular tourist destinations.

Water Sports on the Costa Brava and Costa de la Luz

Tarifa, often dubbed the windsurfing and kiteboarding capital of Spain, is the prime destination for wind-driven water sports. Located at the southern tip of Andalucía, where the Mediterranean meets the Atlantic, the strong winds create perfect conditions for both windsurfing and kiteboarding. The area is renowned for its constant, reliable winds, which attract professionals from around the world to its beaches. Rentals in Tarifa generally cost between €30 and €50 per day, making it accessible for both beginners and advanced riders. For those new to the sport, Tarifa offers plenty of schools and instructors, with lessons typically priced around €40 to €70 for a two-hour session. These lessons are a great way to get started, as instructors cater to all skill levels and teach in some of the best conditions for learning. Tarifa is about a 1.5-hour drive from Málaga, making it an easy day trip for those staying in the region.

Beyond Tarifa, there are other fantastic spots for water sports along the Costa de la Luz, such as Cádiz and Conil de la Frontera. These coastal towns are not only known for their beautiful beaches but also for their excellent wind and wave conditions, making them perfect for windsurfing and kiteboarding. Cádiz, with its wide, sandy beaches, is particularly great for beginners, as the waters tend to be calm and the wind conditions are steady but not overwhelming. Many schools along the coast offer equipment rentals and lessons, where you can enjoy a fun and safe learning experience in some of Spain's most beautiful coastal settings. Whether you're looking for a gentle introduction to windsurfing or kiteboarding, or you want to refine your skills, the Costa de la Luz is a fantastic place to do it.

For those interested in a calmer, more relaxed water sport experience, places like El Palmar are perfect. This small village in the province of Cádiz is home to pristine, clear waters that are ideal for beginners. The gentle waves and calm waters allow newcomers to build confidence in surfing, making El Palmar a great place to start before heading to more challenging spots. The region is also known for its laid-back atmosphere and stunning natural beauty, making it a peaceful retreat for those who want to unwind while enjoying water sports.

In addition to windsurfing and kiteboarding, Andalucía is also a fantastic destination for diving. The waters off Cabo de Gata, in the Almería province, are some of the most pristine in Spain, with an impressive marine ecosystem that makes it one of the country's top diving spots. The Cabo de Gata-Níjar Natural Park is a protected marine reserve, offering divers the chance to explore crystal-clear waters filled with diverse underwater life, including colorful fish, sea turtles, and even the occasional dolphin. Diving tours here typically cost between €40 and €60 per person, depending on the tour and equipment included.

Getting to these water sports hubs is relatively easy. Tarifa is about a 1.5-hour drive from Málaga, making it perfect for a day trip or a longer stay. Cádiz and Conil de la Frontera are about an hour's drive from Tarifa and are easily accessible by car or bus. El Palmar, a peaceful destination for beginners, is also just a short drive from these towns. If you're planning on doing a guided tour or a group activity, many local companies offer transport options as well, so you can leave the logistics to them and focus on the fun.

Packing for a water sports adventure in Andalucía requires a few essentials. If you plan to take lessons or rent equipment, many shops provide everything you need, including wetsuits, boards, and helmets. However, it's always a good idea to bring sunscreen, a hat, and a refillable water bottle to stay hydrated in the sun. If you're diving, don't forget your certification card (if applicable) and a dive computer, though most dive shops provide rental equipment.

Horseback Riding in the Andalusian Countryside

Ronda, a town famous for its dramatic cliffs and historic architecture, offers some of the best horseback riding trails in Andalucía. The paths here wind through rolling hills, olive groves, and vineyards, with panoramic views of the surrounding countryside and the iconic El Tajo gorge. Riding through Ronda's countryside, you'll pass by ancient ruins, hidden villages, and fields of wildflowers, all while enjoying the gentle rhythm of the horse's stride. The area's varied terrain is perfect for both novice and experienced riders, with gentle trails for those just starting out and more challenging routes for seasoned equestrians.

Another excellent region for horseback riding is the Sierra de Grazalema, known for its lush landscapes and rugged mountains. Grazalema, a charming white village nestled in the heart of the park, is surrounded by dramatic cliffs, dense forests, and tranquil rivers, making it an idyllic setting for a horseback adventure. Riders can follow scenic trails that take them through the park's unique ecosystems, offering glimpses of wildlife and unforgettable views of the surrounding peaks. Whether you're trotting through pine forests or galloping along open fields, the Sierra de Grazalema offers a peaceful yet exhilarating experience that's sure to connect you with nature.

For a truly unique adventure, Doñana National Park offers some of the most memorable horseback riding experiences in Andalucía. This UNESCO World Heritage site is home to a vast and diverse ecosystem, including wetlands, dunes, and forests, which makes it a paradise for nature lovers. Riding through Doñana's unique landscape allows you to explore areas that are otherwise difficult to access, where you might spot wild horses, flamingos, or even elusive lynx. Equestrian centers like Centro Ecuestre El Rocío in Huelva offer guided horseback tours through the Doñana wetlands, giving riders the chance to discover the park's breathtaking beauty while learning about its rich biodiversity. The cost of these tours typically ranges from €30 to €80 for a two-hour ride, depending on the location and the guide.

Horseback riding tours are easy to book, with numerous equestrian centers scattered throughout the region. Many of these centers offer a variety of tours, ranging from short rides that last a couple of hours to longer multi-day excursions that take riders through multiple regions. For those new to horseback riding, many centers also provide beginner lessons to help you feel comfortable before heading out on the trails. A basic tour usually includes the horse rental, the guide's expertise, and sometimes refreshments along the way.

When preparing for a horseback riding tour in Andalucía, there are a few key things to keep in mind. It's important to wear long pants and comfortable shoes, as you'll spend several hours in the saddle. A helmet is usually provided by the equestrian center for safety, but it's a good idea to bring your own if you have a preferred one. Sunscreen and a hat are also essential, as the Andalusian sun can be intense, particularly during the warmer months. For longer rides, be sure to bring a water bottle to stay hydrated, especially during the summer heat.

Spring and fall are the best times to visit Andalucía for horseback riding, as the weather is mild and the landscape is particularly beautiful during these seasons. In spring, the countryside comes alive with wildflowers, while fall brings cooler temperatures and stunning autumnal colors. These seasons offer ideal conditions for riding, as the heat of summer can make long rides uncomfortable, especially for beginners.

For a more immersive experience, consider booking a multi-day horseback riding tour. These longer rides often include overnight stays at rural accommodations or riding retreats, allowing you to explore more of Andalucía's breathtaking countryside. Staying in charming rural villages or country estates gives you a deeper connection to the land and a true taste of Andalusian hospitality. These extended tours often follow ancient paths, taking riders through picturesque villages, olive groves, and rolling hills, with plenty of opportunities to rest and soak in the beauty of the landscape.

Chapter 7: Andalucian Cuisine

The Best Tapas Bars

The concept of tapas originated as small portions of food served to accompany drinks, often used to cover the glass to protect it from dust. Over time, these simple bites evolved into an array of delicious dishes that range from cured meats and seafood to hearty stews and fried snacks. In Andalucía, tapas are often served for free with a drink in some establishments, though many places charge for them, especially in more touristy areas. Regardless, tapas remain an affordable and delicious way to explore the local flavors.

One of the best places to experience the essence of tapas is in Seville, the heart of Andalusian cuisine. El Rinconcillo, founded in 1670, is one of the oldest tapas bars in the city and a must-visit for anyone looking to enjoy authentic Andalusian flavors. Known for its rustic charm and traditional atmosphere, El Rinconcillo offers a wide range of tapas, including classics like *jamón ibérico* (cured ham) and *tortilla española* (Spanish omelette). A tapa here typically costs between €2 and €5, making it an affordable spot to indulge in the region's culinary delights. Seville's Triana district is another great area to find excellent tapas bars. Its lively streets are lined with bars offering a variety of traditional and innovative tapas, making it perfect for a tapas crawl.

In Málaga, seafood lovers will find a paradise in the bustling seafood tapas scene. Bar El Tintero, located by the beach in the La Malagueta neighborhood, is famous for its fresh fish and seafood tapas. The experience at El Tintero is unique, with waiters calling out the names of the seafood dishes as they pass by, and customers simply wave them down to make their selection. Prices here range from €5 to €15 per tapa, reflecting the quality of the ingredients. The bar serves everything from *pescaito frito* (fried fish) to grilled sardines, offering a true taste of Málaga's coastal cuisine. La Malagueta is an ideal area to explore for tapas, especially in the evening when the area comes alive with locals enjoying their after-work drinks and small plates.

While each city in Andalucía offers its own take on tapas, some dishes remain staples across the region. *Jamón ibérico*, one of the most famous Spanish delicacies, is often served as thinly sliced pieces of cured ham that melt in your mouth with each bite. *Croquetas*, fried bite-sized balls filled with everything from béchamel sauce to meat or fish, are another beloved tapa that can be found in bars throughout Andalucía. For those craving something lighter, *gazpacho*—a refreshing cold tomato-based soup—is a perfect option, especially during the warmer months.

A typical tapas meal in Andalucía can cost between €10 and €20, depending on the number of dishes ordered and the bar's location. If you're hopping from one bar to another, as locals often do, it's easy to sample a variety of dishes without breaking the bank. Many tapas bars offer a selection of regional wines or local beers that pair beautifully with the food, enhancing the overall experience. It's also important to note that the best time to enjoy tapas in Andalucía is usually in the late afternoon or early evening, when locals head to their favorite bars after work for a drink and a bite to eat. This is when the atmosphere is most vibrant and authentic, with the clinking of glasses and lively conversations filling the air.

To find the best tapas spots in each city, it's best to follow the locals. In Seville, areas like Triana and the historic center are packed with hidden gems, where you can enjoy everything from the most traditional tapas to more modern interpretations. Similarly, in Málaga, La Malagueta and the city's old town offer a mix of traditional seafood tapas bars and innovative eateries that highlight the best of the region's coastal cuisine. The beauty of Andalucía is that there is always something new to discover— whether it's a hidden tavern down a narrow alley or a bustling plaza filled with people savoring their tapas.

Andalusian Wines

The world of Sherry wine is diverse and complex, with several distinct types that each have their own unique flavors and aging processes. The three most popular types of Sherry are Fino, Manzanilla, and Oloroso. Fino is the lightest and driest of the Sherry wines, characterized by its pale color and crisp, dry taste. Manzanilla, often considered a subtype of Fino, is produced in the coastal town of Sanlúcar de Barrameda, and has a slightly saltier, more delicate flavor, thanks to the influence of the nearby sea. Oloroso, on the other hand, is a darker, richer Sherry with a deeper, nuttier flavor. It's typically aged longer than Fino, which gives it a more intense profile with notes of dried fruit and spices.

The process of making Sherry is unique in the world of winemaking. After the grapes are harvested, the wine undergoes a fermentation process, followed by aging in oak barrels. Sherry is aged using a system known as the "solera," where older wines are blended with younger ones to maintain consistency in flavor. The aging process is crucial for the development of Sherry's signature taste. The interaction between the wine and the oak barrels, along with the yeast that forms a protective film on top of the wine during the aging process, plays a key role in shaping the character of each type of Sherry.

One of the best places to experience Sherry firsthand is at Bodegas Tío Pepe in Jerez de la Frontera. This renowned winery offers guided tours that take visitors through the winemaking process, from the vineyards to the oak barrels, and, of course, there's a tasting at the end. Tours start at €10, and you'll have the opportunity to sample different varieties of Sherry, gaining a deeper understanding of the production methods and the distinct qualities of each wine. Jerez de la Frontera is about an hour's drive or train ride from Seville, making it an easy day trip for those looking to immerse themselves in the world of Sherry.

While Sherry may be the star of the show, the Montilla-Moriles region, located just north of Córdoba, is another wine-producing area worth exploring. Known for its sweet and dry wines, Montilla-Moriles produces a range of wines that share similarities with Sherry, but with their own distinct characteristics. The wines here are often made from the Pedro Ximénez grape, which lends a rich sweetness to the wine. Tasting tours in the Montilla-Moriles region typically range from €20 to €30, and they offer a chance to sample the wines alongside the region's unique terroir. If you're in the Córdoba area, it's well worth venturing to Montilla-Moriles for a wine tasting experience.

When visiting Andalucía's cities like Seville or Granada, you'll find plenty of wine bars and bodegas offering a selection of Sherry and other local wines. In Seville, head to the historic Santa Cruz district, where you can enjoy a glass of Fino or Manzanilla, paired with traditional tapas like jamón ibérico or croquetas. In Granada, the Albaicín neighborhood is a great place to find cozy bars serving local wines alongside a variety of tapas. Expect to pay around €3 to €7 per glass, depending on the type of wine and the establishment.

For wine enthusiasts who want to take their experience a step further, consider a day trip or guided wine tour. Companies like Sherry Wine Tours offer guided tastings and tours of the Sherry-producing regions, typically priced between €50 and €80 per person. These tours provide an in-depth look at the history and process of Sherry production, with stops at some of the most famous bodegas in Jerez. For those interested in Montilla-Moriles, there are similar tours that delve into the unique winemaking methods of this lesser-known but equally fascinating region.

Sweet Treats

Churros are perhaps the most beloved sweet treat in Andalucía, especially as a breakfast indulgence. These golden, crispy fried dough sticks are often enjoyed dipped in a rich, velvety hot chocolate. The combination of the hot, slightly bitter chocolate and the warm, doughy churros makes for an irresistible pairing. In Seville, one of the best spots to enjoy this classic treat is Churrería Los Valencianos, where the churros are served fresh and crispy, just as they should be. A serving typically costs between €2 and €5, depending on the size and the number of churros you order. Many locals enjoy churros with a cup of coffee or a thick, sweet chocolate for dipping, making it a popular choice for a morning snack or an afternoon pick-me-up.

Another popular dessert, though not originally from Andalucía, is Tarta de Santiago. This almond-based cake, originating from Galicia, has become a favorite across Spain, especially in the southern regions. With its soft, moist texture and rich almond flavor, Tarta de Santiago is a perfect treat for those with a sweet tooth. The cake is traditionally topped with the cross of Saint James, and its simple yet delicious flavor makes it a favorite for dessert lovers. In Seville, La Mallorquina is an excellent place to sample this regional dessert, where a slice typically costs around €3 to €5. The bakery's version is rich and flavorful, with just the right amount of sweetness, making it a must-try for anyone exploring Seville's sweet offerings.

But Andalucía's sweet repertoire doesn't end there. Turrón, a type of nougat made with almonds and honey, is a popular treat during the holiday season, though it can be found in stores year-round. This dense, sweet confection has its origins in the region of Alicante but is beloved throughout Spain, particularly during Christmas. Turrón can be found in various forms, from the crunchy variety with whole almonds to softer, creamier versions. It's common to pick up a box of turrón as a gift, but it's also a perfect snack for those with a sweet craving.

Another delightful Andalusian pastry is the pionono, a small, sweet roll originating from Santa Fe, a town near Granada. These delicate pastries are made from thin layers of sponge cake, soaked in syrup, and topped with a dollop of whipped cream. The pionono is a simple yet decadent treat, perfect for those who want something sweet but not overwhelming. In Granada, you can find them in most local bakeries, and they are a must-try for any dessert lover visiting the city.

For those looking to explore Andalucía's desserts more extensively, a dessert tour is a fantastic way to indulge in the region's sweetest offerings. Several companies in cities like Seville, Granada, and Córdoba offer guided dessert tours where you can sample a variety of local treats, including churros, tarta de Santiago, piononos, and more. These tours often take you through charming neighborhoods, allowing you to not only enjoy the sweets but also experience the local culture and history along the way.

Finding these treats is easy, as many local bakeries and cafés in Andalucía offer a wide range of traditional and contemporary sweets. In Seville, head to the bustling streets of the city center to find the best churro stands and bakeries offering Tarta de Santiago. In Granada, a stroll through the Albayzín or near the famous Alhambra will lead you to some of the city's best pastry shops where piononos and other regional sweets are sold fresh daily.

Street Food and Markets

In Seville, two of the most popular markets are the Mercado de Triana and the Mercado de la Encarnación. The Mercado de Triana, located in the historic Triana district, is a vibrant spot where locals shop for fresh produce, meats, cheeses, and seafood. It's also a great place to sample some of Seville's iconic street food. Try boquerones, which are freshly fried anchovies, or indulge in a plate of jamón ibérico, the rich and flavorful cured ham that's a staple of Andalusian cuisine. Street food prices here typically range from €3 to €8 per item, making it an affordable and delicious way to dive into local flavors. Nearby, the Mercado de la Encarnación, housed in a striking modern building, offers a similarly rich culinary experience, with tapas-style dishes and traditional Andalusian fare served by friendly market vendors.

For those in Córdoba or Málaga, the Mercado Victoria and the Atarazanas Market offer equally exciting food experiences. Córdoba's Mercado Victoria is a charming and lively market, filled with stalls offering everything from olives to cheeses and cured meats. The market's relaxed atmosphere makes it a perfect spot to wander through, sample local products, and enjoy a glass of local wine paired with a few tapas. The prices here are also reasonable, with most dishes costing between €3 and €8. Málaga's Atarazanas Market is another must-visit for food lovers, especially those craving fresh seafood. You'll find an array of fish and shellfish, from tender calamari to the iconic *pescaito frito* (fried fish), a favorite local dish. Stalls also sell an abundance of local olives, cheeses, and cured meats, which make for perfect snacks as you explore the market.

Navigating the markets is part of the fun. As you stroll through the bustling aisles, be sure to sample a little bit of everything. The best way to enjoy the street food experience is to grab a seat at one of the local stalls or small bars inside the market, where you can relax, sip a cold drink, and savor the flavors at your leisure. Some markets even have designated areas where you can sit and enjoy your food in the company of friends or fellow travelers. If you're unsure about what to try, don't hesitate to ask the vendors for recommendations—they're usually happy to share their knowledge and guide you toward the best local treats.

For those looking to immerse themselves even further into the world of Andalusian street food, joining a food tour can be a great way to experience the markets with the guidance of an expert. Market food tours typically range from €25 to €50 per person and offer a more structured way to explore the region's culinary delights. These tours often include stops at several local markets and food stalls, where you'll learn about the history of the food and the techniques used to prepare it. It's a fun and informative way to get an insider's perspective on Andalusian cuisine while tasting a wide variety of dishes along the way.

The best times to visit markets in Andalucía depend on what kind of experience you're looking for. Early mornings are perfect for those who want to experience the hustle and bustle of the market as it comes to life, with vendors setting up their stalls and locals doing their daily shopping. For a more relaxed atmosphere, late afternoons offer a quieter vibe, with plenty of opportunities to sit down at a stall and enjoy your food at a leisurely pace. It's also a great time to catch the evening crowd, as locals often pop into markets after work for tapas and drinks.

Cooking Classes and Culinary Experiences in Andalucia

In Seville, the culinary heart of Andalucía, there are plenty of opportunities to dive into the region's food scene. La Escuela de Cocina de Seville is a highly recommended school for anyone looking to get hands-on in the kitchen. This school offers classes that focus on a variety of Andalusian specialties, such as paella, salmorejo (a refreshing tomato-based soup), and a range of tapas. Classes here typically cost between €50 and €100 per person, depending on the type of lesson and its duration. The classes are hands-on, allowing you to learn traditional cooking techniques and recreate dishes that are staples of Andalusian cuisine. The school is located in Seville's historic center, making it easy to reach from most parts of the city.

Another popular option for cooking enthusiasts is Bite Me Food Tours, which offers a variety of food-related experiences in Seville, including cooking lessons. These classes typically include a market tour, where you'll visit local markets to select fresh ingredients, followed by a cooking session where you prepare traditional Andalusian dishes under the guidance of an expert chef. Bite Me Food Tours specializes in a more personalized experience, offering both private and group classes. Prices for these sessions generally range from €70 to €100 per person, depending on the length of the tour and the number of participants.

For those looking to specialize in certain aspects of Andalusian cuisine, there are also classes that focus on specific elements of the region's food culture. Olive oil is one of the most important ingredients in Andalusian cooking, and learning how to taste and cook with olive oil can be a fascinating experience. Many culinary schools in Seville offer olive oil tasting workshops, where participants learn about different varieties of olive oil, how to pair them with dishes, and the role olive oil plays in Andalusian cuisine. These classes are perfect for food lovers who want to deepen their appreciation of one of Spain's most famous exports.

Another unique experience for those with a sweet tooth is taking a class on traditional Andalusian desserts. The region has a rich tradition of pastries and sweets, from *tarta de Santiago* (an almond-based cake) to *piononos* (small sponge cakes soaked in syrup). Learning how to make these treats in a local kitchen gives you insight into Andalusian home cooking traditions. There are specialized classes that focus entirely on these desserts, offering hands-on lessons in preparing some of the region's most beloved sweets.

Booking a cooking class in Seville or other Andalusian cities is straightforward, but it's recommended to reserve in advance, especially during peak tourist seasons, as classes can fill up quickly. Many schools allow you to book online or via phone, and the confirmation process is usually quick and easy. As most of these schools are located in the city center, they are easily accessible by foot or public transport, making it convenient to combine a cooking class with sightseeing.

For those seeking a more immersive experience in the Andalusian countryside, there are several cooking retreats and rural cooking schools where you can learn to prepare traditional meals in a more relaxed and intimate setting. These classes often include stays at charming rural accommodations, where you can enjoy meals made with fresh, locally sourced ingredients. Cooking in the countryside gives you a deeper connection to the land and its food, providing a richer understanding of Andalusian traditions. Some of these rural retreats also include hiking, wine tasting, and visits to local markets, offering a more comprehensive culinary experience.

Chapter 8: Where to Stay in Andalucia

Seville

For those seeking the ultimate in luxury, **Hotel Alfonso XIII** is a must. This historic five-star hotel, located near the Seville Cathedral, is one of the most iconic and prestigious hotels in the city. The hotel's grand architecture, which reflects Andalusian, Moorish, and Castilian styles, makes it a destination in itself. Guests are treated to impeccable service, lavish rooms, and a central location that's just a short walk from major attractions like the Alcázar and Plaza de España. Prices at Hotel Alfonso XIII typically range from €200 to €500 per night, depending on the season and room type. While it's a splurge, the experience is unforgettable, and the luxury is second to none.

For those looking for something more intimate but still with high-quality service, **Hotel Casa 1800 Seville** is an excellent choice. Located in the heart of Seville, this boutique hotel offers a unique and charming atmosphere that reflects the city's Moorish influences. The rooms are elegant and spacious, with intricate decor and modern amenities. The hotel is just a short walk from the Seville Cathedral and the Giralda Tower, making it a fantastic base for exploring the city. Prices here are more affordable, starting at around €100 to €150 per night, offering a luxurious experience without the hefty price tag of larger hotels.

If you're looking for something even more intimate, **La Casa del Maestro** in the Santa Cruz district offers a cozy and quaint atmosphere that feels more like staying in a home than a hotel. With its charming décor, personal service, and affordable rates, this bed and breakfast is perfect for those who want to immerse themselves in the local culture. Prices range from €60 to €100 per night, making it a budget-friendly option without compromising on comfort. Staying in the Santa Cruz district means you'll be close to some of Seville's most famous attractions, such as the Alcázar and the Seville Cathedral, all while enjoying the quiet, charming streets of this historic neighborhood.

For travelers who want to experience Seville like a local, **traditional patios** offer a unique and authentic stay. These historic, family-run guesthouses are often located in the heart of the city, with some of them nestled in the picturesque neighborhoods of **Triana** or **Alameda de Hércules**. Staying in a traditional patio gives you a glimpse into Seville's past, with beautiful courtyards surrounded by colorful tiles, lush plants, and a sense of calm that's hard to find in larger hotels. Prices for these guesthouses typically start around €50 to €90 per night, providing a cozy, affordable option with a genuine Andalusian feel.

The location of your accommodation in Seville can greatly enhance your experience, depending on what you're looking to get out of your visit. Staying in the **city center** places you within walking distance of Seville's major attractions, such as the Seville Cathedral, Alcázar, and Plaza de España, making it easy to explore the city's most famous landmarks. The city center also offers plenty of dining and shopping options, so you're never far from a tapas bar or a local market. However, for those seeking a quieter, more authentic experience, neighborhoods like **Triana** provide a more local atmosphere, where you can explore narrow streets, discover hidden bars, and experience a slower pace of life. Triana is across the river from the city center, offering a slightly more residential feel, but still within easy reach of all the main attractions.

Granada

For those seeking an upscale experience, **Parador de Granada** is an exceptional choice. Located within the Alhambra grounds itself, this five-star hotel combines luxury with history. Housed in a former monastery, Parador de Granada offers stunning views of the Alhambra's gardens and the city of Granada. With its elegant rooms and tranquil atmosphere, it's a perfect place to stay if you want to experience the Alhambra up close. Prices here range from €150 to €250 per night, depending on the season and room type. Staying in this historic hotel is an experience in itself, as you'll be able to walk directly from your room into the Alhambra's breathtaking courtyards and gardens.

If you're looking for something a bit more boutique but still close to the Alhambra, **Hotel Alhambra Palace** is an excellent option. This elegant hotel, located just a short walk from the Alhambra, offers panoramic views of the monument and the city. The classic, luxurious design of the hotel gives guests a sense of timeless elegance, with beautifully decorated rooms and an inviting atmosphere. Room rates here start from around €120 to €200 per night, making it an ideal choice for those who want a touch of luxury without going all the way to the five-star price range. The hotel's proximity to the Alhambra makes it convenient for those wanting to visit the site early in the morning or late in the evening when it's quieter.

For a more intimate, local experience, staying in **Albaicín**, the historic district of Granada, is a wonderful option. This area is famous for its narrow, winding streets, whitewashed houses, and views of the Alhambra from every corner. You can find charming guesthouses and small hotels here that offer a more authentic Andalusian feel. One such place is **Carmen de la Alcubilla del Caracol**, a traditional Andalusian house with stunning views of the Alhambra. This small guesthouse offers a more affordable option with rates ranging from €70 to €120 per night. The cozy, rustic charm of Carmen de la Alcubilla del Caracol provides a peaceful retreat while still being close to Granada's main attractions, including the Alhambra.

For those traveling on a tighter budget, **Granada Inn Backpackers** is a great option. Located in the city center, this hostel offers dormitory beds for around €20 to €30 per night, making it one of the most affordable places to stay in the city. It's a lively and social atmosphere, perfect for solo travelers or those on a budget looking for a more communal experience. While it's a bit farther from the Alhambra compared to some other options, the hostel is easily accessible via public transport or a short walk, making it convenient for those who don't mind a bit of a trek.

The best part about staying near the Alhambra, regardless of where you choose to stay, is how easy it is to get around the city. Public transport in Granada is efficient, and there are several buses that can take you up to the Alhambra, especially if you're staying further away. Walking to the Alhambra from most accommodations in the city center is also a pleasant experience, as it allows you to explore the charming streets of Granada, such as the Alcaicería and the Plaza Nueva, while making your way to this stunning monument.

Rural Retreats

One of the most stunning rural retreats in Andalucía is **Finca el Rodeo**, located in the heart of the Sierra de Grazalema Natural Park. This charming rural estate allows guests to truly experience nature, surrounded by dramatic cliffs, rolling hills, and peaceful forests. The finca is a perfect place for those who enjoy hiking, birdwatching, and stargazing, offering countless trails through the surrounding park. Prices here range from €100 to €250 per night, depending on the season, making it a mid-range to high-end option. The tranquil environment, combined with modern comforts, makes Finca el Rodeo an ideal place to recharge and reconnect with nature. The surrounding area is dotted with small villages, such as Grazalema, where you can explore traditional whitewashed houses and sample local delicacies.

For another beautiful rural stay, **Cortijo Las Esquinas** near Ronda is a charming choice that offers rustic allure with modern amenities. This rural hotel, situated in the midst of sprawling olive groves, provides stunning views of the surrounding mountains, allowing guests to enjoy nature from the comfort of their rooms. The hotel is designed to blend in with its environment, featuring traditional Andalusian architecture while ensuring a high level of comfort. With prices ranging from €90 to €180 per night, it's an affordable option for those who want to experience the charm of the Andalusian countryside without breaking the bank. Guests can enjoy various outdoor activities such as hiking, cycling, and horseback riding, making it a perfect destination for those who love to explore the landscape.

For those who want to truly immerse themselves in rural life, **La Cañada de la Virgen** near Antequera offers an authentic farm stay experience. This working farm gives visitors the opportunity to engage in the daily activities of farm life, from milking cows to collecting eggs. The experience is both educational and immersive, providing a unique insight into traditional Andalusian agriculture. Prices for a stay at La Cañada de la Virgen start from around €80 per night, making it one of the more affordable rural retreats. The farm's location, surrounded by fields and olive groves, offers plenty of space for hiking and exploring, while the starry night skies provide the perfect setting for stargazing.

Staying in these rural properties offers a serene experience that's hard to find in more touristy areas. The slower pace of life in the countryside allows you to unwind, breathe in the fresh air, and enjoy the natural beauty of Andalucía. Whether you're enjoying a quiet morning on your private terrace, taking a walk through the olive orchards, or watching the sunset over the mountains, these rural retreats offer an unmatched sense of tranquility.

To get to these rural accommodations, a car is often the best mode of transport, as they tend to be located outside of major towns and require a bit of a drive. Many rural properties provide private parking, which makes it easy to explore the surrounding areas at your own pace. Whether you're heading to the stunning villages of the Sierra de Grazalema or venturing out to the ancient city of Ronda, a car gives you the freedom to explore the region's rural charms.

In addition to the natural beauty of the countryside, many rural retreats also offer opportunities for outdoor activities. Hiking and cycling are popular options, with numerous trails that weave through the scenic landscapes of Andalucía. Some properties even offer guided tours or activities such as cooking classes, wine tasting, or olive oil tours, allowing you to experience local traditions firsthand. The slower, quieter environment is also perfect for stargazing, as rural areas often have minimal light pollution, giving you a chance to see the night sky in all its glory.

Beachfront Escapes on the Costa del Sol

For an unforgettable luxury experience, **Hotel Los Monteros** in Marbella is a top choice. This five-star hotel, located just a short drive from the Marbella city center, offers direct access to a private beach, ensuring guests enjoy an exclusive and serene beachfront experience. The hotel's elegant rooms and suites are designed with sophistication in mind, offering spacious accommodations with stunning sea views. With prices starting at €200 per night, it's perfect for those looking to experience the height of luxury in one of the most prestigious areas on the Costa del Sol.

If you're looking to stay near the iconic **Puerto Banús**, famous for its high-end shopping and vibrant nightlife, **Gran Hotel Guadalpin Banus** is another excellent option. This hotel offers everything you'd expect from a luxury beachfront resort, including a beautiful pool, fine dining, and easy access to the beach. With rates ranging from €150 to €300 per night, it offers a range of options for those wanting to indulge in luxury while staying in one of the Costa del Sol's most glamorous areas. Puerto Banús is also a hub for yacht enthusiasts, so you can expect to see some impressive boats docked in the marina as you stroll along the coast.

For those seeking a more affordable stay without sacrificing the beachfront location, **Hotel Sur Málaga** in Torremolinos offers a great value. This mid-range hotel is just a short walk from the beach, making it perfect for guests who want easy access to the sea without paying premium prices. Rates start from €80 per night, making it a great choice for travelers looking for a budget-friendly yet comfortable option. Torremolinos is a lively town with a variety of shops, restaurants, and bars, making it ideal for those who want to combine beach relaxation with a little more activity.

If you're in the mood for a more relaxed, chic beach experience, **La Plage Casanis** in Estepona offers a laid-back vibe with a stylish touch. This boutique hotel combines modern décor with coastal charm, providing guests with a cozy yet sophisticated environment. Located just a short distance from the beach, guests can enjoy an easygoing atmosphere while still being close to the shoreline. Prices at La Plage Casanis start at €100 per night, making it an ideal choice for those who prefer a quieter, more intimate stay without the high price tag. Estepona itself is a charming town with a beautiful seafront promenade and plenty of quaint restaurants and cafés to enjoy.

Booking beachfront accommodations on the Costa del Sol, especially during the summer months, requires some planning. These hotels are in high demand, and many offer limited availability during peak seasons, so it's wise to book early to secure the best rates and preferred room types. If you're looking to stay in a specific area, such as Marbella or Estepona, try to reserve several months in advance to ensure you get the most convenient location.

While the beaches and resorts of the Costa del Sol are the main attraction, there are plenty of nearby sights worth exploring. **Málaga**, the regional capital, is just a short drive away and offers a wealth of historical and cultural attractions, including the Picasso Museum, the Alcazaba fortress, and the vibrant old town. For those who enjoy a bit of adventure, **Ronda**, perched high in the mountains, is a picturesque town with dramatic views and historic charm. And for a more traditional Andalusian experience, **Mijas**, a charming hilltop village, offers narrow winding streets, whitewashed houses, and stunning vistas of the Mediterranean.

Budget Travel

For those visiting **Seville**, one of the most affordable yet comfortable options is **Ibis Seville**, a budget-friendly hotel located in the heart of the city. With modern rooms, free Wi-Fi, and a central location just a short walk from the major attractions like the Seville Cathedral and Alcázar, Ibis offers excellent value for money. Rates typically range from €50 to €80 per night, making it a perfect choice for travelers who want to explore the city without overspending. The hotel's simple, no-frills approach to comfort ensures a pleasant stay without compromising on convenience.

If you're looking for a more social and vibrant atmosphere, **The Nomad Hostel** in **Málaga** is a great option. Known for its clean facilities, friendly staff, and welcoming environment, this hostel offers a great budget-friendly choice for solo travelers or those looking to meet fellow explorers. Dormitory beds start at around €15 to €30 per night, making it one of the most affordable options in the city. The Nomad Hostel's central location means you're within walking distance of Málaga's beautiful beaches, bustling port area, and historic sites like the Alcazaba and Picasso Museum. Staying in a hostel like this also provides a more immersive, local experience, giving you the chance to connect with travelers from around the world.

For a more local and family-friendly experience, **Pensión La Orozca** in **Córdoba** is an excellent choice. This charming, family-run guesthouse offers a cozy and intimate atmosphere, perfect for those who want to experience the warmth of Andalusian hospitality. With rates starting from €40 to €70 per night, Pensión La Orozca provides great value in a fantastic location, just a short walk from the Mezquita and other major attractions in Córdoba's historic center. The small, personalized touches and peaceful ambiance make it a great place to relax after a day of exploring.

If you prefer a more independent stay with the option to cook your own meals, **Apartamentos Jardines de Murillo** in **Seville** offers self-catering apartments at affordable rates. Prices for fully equipped apartments start at €60 to €100 per night, which is ideal for those who want to save money by preparing their own food. The apartments are located near the famous Murillo Gardens and offer easy access to the city center. This is a great option for families or travelers planning a longer stay in Seville, as it provides both comfort and the flexibility to enjoy meals at your own convenience.

When it comes to finding budget-friendly stays in Andalucía, booking in advance can make a significant difference in securing the best rates. Many budget accommodations offer discounts for early reservations, so planning ahead can ensure you get the best value. Another way to save money is by choosing accommodations just outside the city center. While staying in the heart of cities like Seville, Córdoba, or Málaga offers convenience, accommodations a little further out tend to be cheaper, while still providing easy access to the main attractions via public transport or a short walk.

Staying in hostels or guesthouses also offers the added benefit of a more immersive experience. These types of accommodations tend to have a more personal feel, with the opportunity to interact with locals and other travelers. Many hostels organize tours, events, and group activities, which can be a great way to explore the area and meet new people. Similarly, guesthouses like **Pensión La Orozca** provide a more intimate setting where you can experience Andalusian hospitality firsthand.

Chapter 9: Andalucian Day Trips and Hidden Gems

Day Trips From Seville

One of the most accessible and rewarding day trips from Seville is a visit to the Roman ruins of **Itálica**, located just 20 minutes from the city by car or bus. Itálica was once a thriving Roman city and is now one of Spain's most well-preserved archaeological sites. The ruins include a grand amphitheater, which once hosted gladiator games and could hold up to 25,000 spectators. You can also admire the intricate mosaics that adorn the floors of the ancient houses. The site offers a fascinating glimpse into life during Roman times, and at just €1.50 for entry, it's an affordable and enriching experience. Itálica's proximity to Seville makes it an ideal half-day trip for those looking to explore beyond the city's limits while still being close enough for an easy return.

For a change of pace and a scenic escape, consider visiting the **White Villages** (Pueblos Blancos), a series of charming towns known for their narrow streets, whitewashed buildings, and traditional Andalusian atmosphere. The **village of Ronda** is one of the most famous, sitting dramatically atop a deep gorge and offering stunning views of the surrounding mountains. It's about a 1.5-hour drive or bus ride from Seville, making it an easy day trip. In Ronda, the must-see attraction is the **Puente Nuevo**, the impressive 18th-century bridge that spans the El Tajo gorge. Walking across the bridge offers breathtaking views of the valley below. The town is also home to the **Plaza de Toros**, one of the oldest bullrings in Spain, which is worth visiting to understand the history of bullfighting in Andalusia.

If you're looking to explore more of the natural beauty of Andalucía, the **Grazalema Natural Park** is a peaceful retreat just an hour's drive from Ronda. Known for its lush landscapes, dramatic cliffs, and rich biodiversity, the park offers excellent opportunities for hiking and nature walks. Whether you're strolling through pine forests or taking in panoramic mountain views, Grazalema is a great place to unwind and enjoy the outdoors. The park is free to visit, so it's an affordable way to immerse yourself in the natural beauty of the region.

Another charming town in the area is **Arcos de la Frontera**, one of the most stunning Pueblos Blancos. Perched on a cliff, Arcos offers sweeping views of the surrounding countryside and is a delightful place to wander through narrow cobbled streets lined with whitewashed houses and flower-filled balconies. The town is rich in history, with a castle and several historic churches to explore. It's a quieter alternative to Ronda, perfect for travelers looking to experience a more laid-back slice of Andalusian life.

Dining in these villages is an experience in itself, with plenty of local restaurants serving traditional Andalusian cuisine. You can expect hearty meals that reflect the region's agricultural roots, such as *puchero* (a meat and vegetable stew) or *jamón ibérico* (cured ham). A typical meal will cost between €10 and €20 per person, depending on the restaurant and the number of dishes you order. In places like Ronda and Grazalema, you'll find many eateries offering outdoor seating, so you can enjoy your meal while taking in the picturesque surroundings.

To get the most out of your visit to the White Villages, consider taking a guided tour. A group tour typically costs between €30 and €50, and it's a great way to learn about the history, culture, and traditions of these enchanting towns. Guides can offer insights into the architecture, the local way of life, and the significance of the region's natural landscapes, enhancing your experience and making the trip even more memorable.

Exploring the Caves of Nerja

The Caves of Nerja (Cueva de Nerja) are one of Andalucía's most captivating natural attractions, making them a perfect day trip for those staying in Málaga or Seville. Located about 1.5 hours by car from Seville, these impressive caves offer a rare chance to explore the underground world of stalactites, stalagmites, and prehistoric art. As you step into the caves, you're not just witnessing natural beauty—you're stepping back in time to an era when early humans painted on the cave walls, leaving behind art that still fascinates us today.

The caves are famous for their enormous size and incredible acoustics, which make it a popular spot for the **Nerja Cave Festival** held annually in the summer. During this time, the caves are transformed into a unique venue for live performances, ranging from classical music to flamenco. The natural acoustics of the cave amplify the music, creating an unforgettable experience. If you plan to visit during the summer, it's worth checking out the festival schedule for a truly one-of-a-kind experience.

As for the cost, entry to the Caves of Nerja is quite affordable, with tickets for adults typically ranging from €10 to €12. A guided tour is included with the entry fee, and the tour lasts about 30 to 40 minutes. The guides provide interesting insights into the history of the caves, explaining the geological formations and the significance of the prehistoric paintings that adorn the cave walls. These paintings, which date back more than 40,000 years, provide a fascinating glimpse into the lives of the ancient peoples who once inhabited the area.

The caves themselves are a marvel, with towering stalactites and stalagmites that have formed over millennia. The intricate shapes and sizes of the formations create an awe-inspiring landscape beneath the earth's surface. Some of the chambers are so large that they could easily fit a small cathedral, and walking through them feels like being inside a natural cathedral of stone.

After your visit to the caves, you can head to **Playa de Burriana**, a beautiful beach just a 10-minute drive from the caves. This scenic beach is the perfect place to relax and unwind after exploring the underground wonders of Nerja. With its clear blue waters, golden sand, and plenty of beachfront restaurants, it offers a peaceful place to enjoy the Mediterranean climate. You can grab a bite to eat, sip a refreshing drink, or simply soak up the sun before heading back to your base.

For those traveling by public transport, there are buses from **Málaga** to **Nerja**, though they can be somewhat limited in terms of frequency and timing. It's a good option for those who prefer not to drive, but for greater flexibility, renting a car is highly recommended. The drive from Málaga to Nerja is scenic and straightforward, and having a car gives you the freedom to explore the town and surrounding areas at your own pace. You can easily visit the caves, relax at the beach, and perhaps explore the charming town of Nerja, all without worrying about bus schedules.

The Hidden Beauty of Ronda and Its Gorge

Ronda is one of Andalucía's most stunning and historic towns, perched dramatically over the deep Tajo Gorge, offering some of the most breathtaking views in the region. This charming town, with its ancient bridges, narrow streets, and rich history, is a must-visit destination for anyone traveling through southern Spain. Ronda's unique location, sitting high above the gorge, creates a sense of awe as you explore the town's fascinating landmarks and scenic viewpoints.

At the heart of Ronda's iconic landscape is the **Puente Nuevo** bridge, which spans the Tajo Gorge, connecting the old town with the newer parts of the city. The bridge itself is an engineering marvel, completed in the late 18th century, and offers some of the most spectacular views of the surrounding valley. Standing on the bridge, you can look down into the gorge, marveling at the dramatic drop below and the river that winds through the base of the canyon. The views from here are a highlight of any trip to Ronda and are especially stunning at sunset, when the town and bridge glow in the warm light.

Another landmark worth visiting is **Plaza de Toros**, one of the oldest bullrings in Spain, which dates back to the late 18th century. Ronda has a rich history with bullfighting, and the bullring remains a significant cultural site. The bullring is still used for events, though you can also take a guided tour to learn about the history of bullfighting in Ronda and see the museum housed within the ring. Tickets for entry typically range from €8 to €12, depending on whether you're just visiting or participating in a guided tour. Whether you're a fan of the sport or simply interested in Ronda's cultural heritage, the Plaza de Toros is an important stop on your journey through the town.

For those who enjoy hiking and the great outdoors, Ronda also offers some fantastic walking routes, such as the **Boca del Asno** trail. This relatively easy hike takes you along the edge of the gorge, offering panoramic views of the surrounding landscape and the town below. The trail is free to access and provides an excellent way to experience the natural beauty of Ronda's surroundings. The hike is particularly scenic, as it winds through lush forests and alongside the river, with plenty of spots to stop and take in the view. It's a perfect way to combine nature with the history of Ronda, offering a peaceful escape from the town's more touristy areas.

Getting to Ronda is simple, with a 2-hour drive or bus ride from Seville. The town is well-connected by road, and the journey itself offers beautiful views of the Andalusian countryside. Once you arrive, you'll find that the town's historic streets are best explored on foot. The old town, with its cobbled lanes and charming plazas, is home to a variety of local shops selling traditional crafts, such as leather goods, ceramics, and, of course, **serrano ham**, which is a specialty of the region. A walk through these streets gives you a sense of the town's rich cultural heritage and provides plenty of opportunities to pick up souvenirs or stop for a coffee at a local café.

Ronda is also a great place to sample local Andalusian cuisine. **Rabo de toro**, a rich oxtail stew, is a traditional dish you'll find at many of the town's cozy restaurants. This hearty dish, slow-cooked to perfection, is perfect for a chilly evening and pairs wonderfully with a glass of local red wine. A typical meal at one of Ronda's charming restaurants will cost between €12 and €25 per person, depending on where you choose to eat. The town is known for its welcoming atmosphere, and many of the local establishments offer outdoor seating, allowing you to enjoy your meal while taking in the spectacular views of the gorge.

Guadalquivir River Cruises

Taking a Guadalquivir River cruise offers a serene and picturesque way to experience Andalucía's cities and landscapes from a unique vantage point. The river flows through the heart of Seville, providing stunning views of the city's most iconic landmarks, while also offering a tranquil escape from the hustle and bustle of daily life.

In Seville, a **Sevilla Boat Tour** is one of the most popular options for a relaxed and scenic river experience. These 1-hour boat tours provide guests with panoramic views of Seville's major landmarks, including the **Torre del Oro**, an iconic watchtower that dates back to the 13th century, and the **Plaza de España**, a stunning square built for the Ibero-American Exposition of 1929. As you glide down the Guadalquivir River, you'll also catch glimpses of the vibrant Triana neighborhood, the colorful riverside, and the lush greenery that lines the water's edge. These cruises are an ideal way to get a fresh perspective of Seville's stunning architecture, and with prices ranging from €15 to €25 per person, they offer great value for a one-hour outing.

For those seeking a more luxurious experience, consider an **evening sunset cruise**, which combines beautiful views of the city with dinner or drinks on board. These cruises provide the perfect setting for a romantic evening, as you sail along the Guadalquivir River at sunset, watching the sky change colors over the city's skyline. During the cruise, you can enjoy a delicious meal or sip a glass of wine while taking in the sights. Prices for these more intimate cruises generally range from €40 to €70 per person, depending on the inclusions and duration. It's an unforgettable experience for anyone looking to explore Seville in style.

Booking a river cruise in Seville is easy, with tickets available both online and at the dock. If you're planning on taking a boat tour, it's always a good idea to reserve in advance, especially during the high tourist season, to secure your preferred time slot. Many tour operators offer departures throughout the day, with evening cruises becoming particularly popular as the temperatures cool and the city lights begin to sparkle.

While Seville may be the most famous city on the Guadalquivir River, the river also flows through other charming Andalusian cities, such as **Córdoba** and **Málaga**, where visitors can enjoy scenic views of the river and the surrounding landscapes. In Córdoba, boat tours offer a peaceful way to see the city from a different angle, where you can enjoy views of the historic **Roman Bridge** and the beautiful gardens along the water. These shorter cruises typically focus on the city's history, offering a relaxing way to learn about Córdoba's past while taking in the surrounding nature.

In **Málaga**, the Guadalquivir River is less central, but cruises in the area offer a chance to explore Málaga's coastal beauty and picturesque landscapes. Here, the tours are more focused on the river's connection to the Mediterranean, as well as the lush natural surroundings of the region. Cruises in Málaga are ideal for those who want to experience a quieter, less touristy part of the river.

For those with more time and a desire to explore Andalucía at a leisurely pace, the **Guadalquivir River** itself stretches through multiple towns, from Seville down to Cádiz. This provides an excellent opportunity to explore the region's rural charm, where the river winds through lush farmland and peaceful countryside. Taking a longer cruise along the river is a wonderful way to see towns like **La Puebla de Cazalla**, **Écija**, and **Sanlúcar de Barrameda**, where you can enjoy the peacefulness of the countryside while learning about local traditions and history.

Chapter 10: Travel Tips for Andalucia

Safety Tips for Traveling Around Andalucia

Andalucía is one of Spain's most welcoming regions, known for its friendly locals and relaxed pace of life. For the most part, it's a safe place to explore, even for solo travelers. Still, as with any destination, staying alert and prepared makes for a smoother experience.

In busy areas like Seville's Plaza de España, Granada's Alhambra entrance, or Málaga's La Malagueta beach, it's wise to be cautious with your belongings. Petty theft is rare but not unheard of, especially in peak tourist seasons. Use a cross-body bag with a secure zipper, keep your phone tucked away in crowds, and don't leave personal items unattended, even at café tables.

When out at night, Andalucía is generally safe, and most town centers stay lively well into the evening. However, if you're walking alone after dark—especially in quieter residential areas outside city centers—stick to well-lit streets and avoid alleys or poorly lit shortcuts. Taxis are available late into the night, but it's better to use apps like **Cabify** or **Uber**, which give you a clear price and route before you ride, helping you avoid overcharging or confusion with unfamiliar pricing systems.

One scam to be aware of involves unofficial taxi drivers at transport hubs who may try to charge double or triple the normal fare. Licensed taxis in Andalucía are white with a green stripe and have a meter. If you're ever in doubt, pre-booking through an app or asking your hotel for a trusted number is the safest option.

In more remote or rural areas, such as **hiking in the Sierra Nevada**, **Grazalema**, or **Doñana National Park**, your safety depends on preparation. Trails are stunning, but mobile signal can be patchy, and some routes are long and exposed. Bring plenty of water, snacks, a basic first aid kit, and good hiking shoes. Always check the weather forecast beforehand—it can change quickly in the mountains—and let someone know your planned route and estimated return time. If you're heading out solo, it's smart to join a local hiking group or book a guided tour.

Solo travelers—particularly women—generally find Andalucía to be comfortable and safe. It's not uncommon to see people walking alone, dining solo, or sightseeing independently. For peace of mind, stick to central neighborhoods like **Santa Cruz in Seville**, **Albaicín in Granada**, or **Soho in Málaga**, and choose accommodation with good reviews. If you're planning to join a tour or excursion, book through reputable operators or tourist offices. Be cautious of people offering informal tours on the street, especially around major attractions.

Health-wise, Andalucía's hot summers can catch travelers off guard. It's not just about heat—it's the intensity of the sun. Even in the shoulder months of May and September, UV levels are high. Apply sunscreen regularly, wear a hat and sunglasses, and try to schedule outdoor activities early in the morning or late afternoon. Tap water is safe to drink across the region, but if you're spending a full day out, carry more than you think you'll need, particularly in rural or hiking areas.

In case of emergencies, dial **112**, which connects to Spain's general emergency services. Most staff in hospitals and major clinics speak at least some English, and pharmacies are widely available in towns and cities.

How to Get Around

Public Transport in Cities

In Seville, the public transport system is both affordable and efficient. The city is well-served by buses and a metro network that connects key locations, including major attractions like the **Alcázar** and **Plaza de España**. A bus or metro ride costs around €1.40 per journey, making it a cost-effective option for tourists who want to explore Seville's many historic sites. The buses are frequent, clean, and easy to navigate, and the metro, while more limited in scope, covers the city's main areas, including the Santa Justa train station. For travelers staying within the city center, walking is often just as convenient, but if you plan to travel further afield or to attractions on the outskirts, public transport is a solid choice.

Seville's **Renfe** train network also connects the city to other Andalusian destinations, offering a comfortable and fast way to travel between cities. High-speed **AVE** trains are the best option for long-distance travel, linking cities like Seville, Granada, and Málaga in just a few hours. The prices for Renfe tickets vary depending on the route and class, with prices generally starting from €20 to €70. For instance, the journey from Seville to

Granada typically takes about two and a half hours, making it a convenient day trip option. Tickets can be purchased online or at the train station, and it's advisable to book in advance, especially for popular routes during peak tourist seasons.

Car Rentals for Rural Exploration

While public transport works well in cities, **renting a car** is the best way to explore Andalucía's more remote and rural areas, including the **White Villages** (Pueblos Blancos) and the natural parks like **Sierra de Grazalema** and **Doñana National Park**. Renting a car gives you the freedom to travel at your own pace and visit less accessible spots that public transport can't reach. For example, towns like **Ronda**, **Grazalema**, and **Mijas** are nestled in the hills and are best accessed by car.

Rental prices typically range from €25 to €60 per day, depending on the type of car you choose. If you're planning to rent a car, it's important to remember that Spain drives on the right-hand side of the road. If you're coming from outside the European Union, you may need an **International Driver's Permit** (IDP) in addition to your home country's driver's license. Be sure to check if your rental company requires it.

While driving in Andalucía is generally easy, navigating parking can sometimes be tricky, especially in city centers and historic districts. In cities like Seville and Málaga, parking is limited and often pricey, so it's wise to check parking availability or use public parking lots. In the countryside, parking is typically easier to find, though in small towns, you might encounter narrow streets and limited space.

Taxis and Rideshare Services

If you're not keen on public transport or renting a car, **taxis** and **rideshare services** like **Uber** and **Cabify** offer convenient alternatives in major cities. Taxi fares typically start at €3 to €5 for short trips within the city, and the rates increase depending on the distance traveled. You can easily hail a taxi in most city centers or find one at designated taxi stands.

Rideshare services like Uber and Cabify operate in Seville, Málaga, and other larger cities, providing an easy way to get around without the need to negotiate taxi fares. They often offer a more transparent pricing system, and you can track your ride, which is especially handy if you're unfamiliar with the area. Though slightly more expensive than public transport, these services are ideal for those who prefer a more comfortable, door-to-door travel option.

Andalucian Customs and Etiquette

To fully appreciate Andalucía, it's important to understand the region's customs and etiquette. Greetings can vary—handshakes are common in formal settings, while **besos** (kisses on both cheeks) are the norm between friends and acquaintances.

When it comes to dining, meals are typically relaxed, with lunch starting around 2 pm and lasting a couple of hours. In many smaller towns, the **siesta** tradition still holds strong, and you'll find businesses closing between 2-5 pm.

Flamenco performances are an essential part of Andalusian culture. During these shows, audiences are expected to be quiet and respectful, giving full attention to the performers. Tipping in restaurants is not mandatory but appreciated, usually around 5-10% of the bill.

Finally, when visiting religious sites, it's important to dress modestly—covering your shoulders and avoiding shorts is generally required in churches and cathedrals. By following these customs, you'll enhance your experience and show respect for Andalusian traditions.

Staying Connected

Staying connected in Andalucía is simple, with plenty of options for SIM cards, Wi-Fi, and internet access across the region. For tourists, a **SIM card** is a convenient choice for mobile data and calls. Major carriers like **Movistar**, **Vodafone**, and **Orange** offer SIM cards at airports, mobile stores, and convenience shops, typically costing between €10 and €20, depending on the data package. These SIM cards are an easy way to stay connected, whether for navigation or staying in touch with family and friends.

In urban centers like **Seville** and **Málaga**, Wi-Fi is widely available in most hotels, cafes, and restaurants. Many places offer free internet access, making it easy to stay connected while enjoying a coffee or a meal. For those who need a more reliable internet connection, renting a **portable Wi-Fi device** is an option, with prices around €5 to €10 per day. These can be rented at airports or booked online ahead of time.

Apps like **Google Maps** and **TripAdvisor** are particularly useful for navigating the cities and finding great restaurant recommendations. Just keep in mind that international roaming charges may apply if you're using services outside the European Union. For a seamless experience, it's best to either use a local SIM or rent a portable Wi-Fi device during your trip.

Useful Phrases to Know

While many people in Andalucía speak English, learning a few basic Spanish phrases can enhance your experience and help you feel more connected to the local culture. Here are some essential phrases to get you started:

Greetings

- Hola (Hello)
- Buenos días (Good morning)
- Buenas tardes (Good afternoon)
- Buenas noches (Good evening / Good night)
- ¿Cómo estás? (How are you?)

Dining and Eating Out

- Una mesa para dos, por favor (A table for two, please)
- ¿Cuánto cuesta? (How much does it cost?)
- La cuenta, por favor (The bill, please)
- ¿Tienen menú en inglés? (Do you have a menu in English?)
- ¿Qué recomienda? (What do you recommend?)

Polite Phrases

- Gracias (Thank you)
- Por favor (Please)
- Perdón/disculpa (Excuse me)

- Lo siento (I'm sorry)
- De nada (You're welcome)

Asking for Directions or Information

- ¿Dónde está…? (Where is…?)
- ¿Habla inglés? (Do you speak English?)
- ¿Cómo llego a…? (How do I get to…?)
- ¿A qué hora abre/cierra? (What time does it open/close?)

Numbers (1-10)

- Uno (1)
- Dos (2)
- Tres (3)
- Cuatro (4)
- Cinco (5)
- Seis (6)
- Siete (7)
- Ocho (8)
- Nueve (9)
- Diez (10)

Other Useful Phrases

- ¿Cuánto tiempo se tarda? (How long does it take?)
- ¿Me puede ayudar? (Can you help me?)
- ¿Dónde está el baño? (Where is the bathroom?)

By learning these simple phrases, you'll make your trip to Andalucía more enjoyable and immersive. It's always appreciated by locals when you make an effort to speak their language, even if it's just a few words!

Emergency Numbers and Health Services

Emergency Numbers

- 112 – General emergency services (ambulance, police, fire)
- 061 – Medical emergency (ambulance services)
- 092 – Local police
- 091 – National police
- 080 – Fire services
- 116 000 – Missing children (national hotline)

Health Services

- Hospital Universitario Virgen del Rocío (Seville) – A leading hospital in Seville.

- Hospital Clínico San Cecilio (Granada) – Another major healthcare facility.

Pharmacies

- **Farmacia** – Pharmacies are widely available throughout Andalucía, and most pharmacies offer emergency service for medication outside normal hours.

  - Pharmacies often display a sign with their hours and the 24-hour pharmacy on duty at a given time.

Travel Health Insurance

- **European Health Insurance Card (EHIC)** – EU residents can access public healthcare in Spain at reduced costs or for free if they have an EHIC card. Always carry it when traveling.

- **Private Travel Insurance** – It's highly recommended to have travel insurance that covers health services, including emergency medical treatment, hospital stays, and medical repatriation.

Ambulance and Medical Assistance

- **Ambulance Services** – Dial **061** for medical assistance or if you require an ambulance to your location.

- **Private Medical Clinics** – There are private clinics throughout Andalucía, with services ranging from general medicine to specialized treatments. Most major cities, including Seville, Málaga, and Granada, have well-regarded private hospitals.

Language Assistance

Medical Interpreters – In some areas, especially tourist-heavy cities like Seville or Málaga, medical professionals may speak English. However, in more rural areas, an interpreter service may be needed if you don't speak Spanish. Check with your hotel or local tourist information centers for available services.

Andalucia's Public Holidays and Festivals

Festival/Event	Date	Location
New Year's Day	January 1	All of Andalucía
Epiphany	January 6	All of Andalucía

Semana Santa (Holy Week)	March/April (dates vary)	Seville, Málaga, Córdoba
Labour Day (Fiesta del Trabajo)	May 1	All of Andalucía
Feria de Abril (Seville Fair)	April (two weeks after Easter)	Seville
May Crosses Festival (Fiesta de las Cruces de Mayo)	May 3	Córdoba, Granada
Corpus Christi	June (dates vary)	Seville, Granada, Jaén
San Juan Night (Noche de San Juan)	June 23	Málaga, Almería
Feria de Agosto (Málaga Fair)	August (mid-August)	Málaga
La Feria de Ronda	August (week of the 23rd)	Ronda
Day of Andalucía	February 28	All of Andalucía
Dia de la Hispanidad	October 12	All of Andalucía
Christmas Day	December 25	All of Andalucía
New Year's Eve (Nochevieja)	December 31	All of Andalucía –
Feria de Jerez	May (first week)	Jerez de la Frontera

Conclusion

Andalucía is a place like no other, where the rhythms of flamenco echo through vibrant cities, the scent of fresh tapas fills the air, and the sun casts a golden glow on stunning landscapes. It's a region that weaves together an incredible tapestry of history, culture, and natural beauty, offering unforgettable experiences at every turn.

From the sun-kissed beaches of the Costa del Sol to the rugged peaks of the Sierra Nevada, Andalucía's landscapes are as diverse as they are breathtaking. The lush countryside, dotted with charming white villages, provides the perfect escape for those looking to reconnect with nature and find peace in the tranquil surroundings.

But Andalucía's magic is not just in its landscapes—it's in its history and the way it blends cultures and traditions. Cities like

Seville, Granada, and Córdoba are steeped in centuries of stories, where Moorish architecture meets Christian heritage, and modern influences add their own vibrant touch. The Alhambra in Granada, the Alcázar in Seville, and the Mezquita in Córdoba are just the beginning. The region's rich history can be felt in every cobblestone street, every ancient monument, and every conversation with the warm-hearted locals.

Andalucía's cities offer a fascinating mix of history, art, and cuisine. Seville's flamenco-filled nights, Granada's stunning palaces, and Córdoba's grand mosques invite exploration at every corner. At the same time, Andalucía's smaller towns offer intimate escapes where you can savor the simpler pleasures of life—whether it's wandering through a sleepy village, enjoying a glass of sherry in Jerez, or discovering ancient ruins in Ronda.

Throughout your journey, take time to immerse yourself in the region's rich culture. Savor every bite of jamón ibérico, taste the sweet simplicity of gazpacho, and allow yourself to be swept away by the passion of a flamenco performance. It's not just about visiting Andalucía—it's about truly experiencing it, from the warmth of its people to the beauty of its landscapes.

As you venture through Andalucía, remember that this is a place to be felt, not just seen. The region invites you to explore its rich heritage, savor its flavors, and engage with its vibrant traditions. Whether you're lost in the alleys of Seville, hiking the paths of the Sierra Nevada, or simply enjoying a sunset over the Alhambra, Andalucía will stay with you long after you leave. So, take a deep breath, soak in every moment, and get ready to embark on an adventure that will leave you forever enchanted by the magic of Andalucía.

Printed in Dunstable, United Kingdom

77245972R00077